Damned if I Do,
Dead if I Don't

Damned if I Do, Dead if I Don't

WRITTEN BY:
HANNAH BONDE

AuthorHouse™
1663 Liberty Drive
Bloomington, IN 47403
www.authorhouse.com
Phone: 1-800-839-8640

© *2011 by Hannah Bonde. All rights reserved.*

No part of this book may be reproduced, stored in a retrieval system, or transmitted by any means without the written permission of the author.

First published by AuthorHouse   09/28/2011

ISBN: 978-1-4670-3730-3 (sc)
ISBN: 978-1-4670-3729-7 (hc)
ISBN: 978-1-4670-3728-0 (ebk)

Library of Congress Control Number: 2011916627

Printed in the United States of America

Any people depicted in stock imagery provided by Thinkstock are models, and such images are being used for illustrative purposes only.
Certain stock imagery © *Thinkstock.*

This book is printed on acid-free paper.

Because of the dynamic nature of the Internet, any web addresses or links contained in this book may have changed since publication and may no longer be valid. The views expressed in this work are solely those of the author and do not necessarily reflect the views of the publisher, and the publisher hereby disclaims any responsibility for them.

MY FIRST 6 YEARS, THE ONLY TIME I HAD A REAL FAMILY

Bang! I just cut the corner and ran right into this six foot blond guy. I was just about to say,
'Watch where you are going!' When I looked up and into the most beautiful eyes I had ever seen. I got a tingle in my body. My cheeks flushed red and all I managed to say was a shy . . .

"Hi."

Those same eyes that held so much promise now filled me with nothing but fear and terror. For the first time I could see clearly that I had to leave him. He will never change. If I stay, I will end up dead!

I was now ready to leave him but that option wouldn't be easy. When I leave, I need to leave the country and my family in order to stay alive. I will have to find a way to escape from him because he will never let me go. I take that back, he would let me go, if I left in a casket or if I were dead.

Deep down, I already had the answer. I knew what I needed to do, but I took my time to ponder my moves and to plan, and let it sink in. I was planning my escape from him and this nightmare. A plan to save my life! But I jumped ahead in this tall, terrible tale, so let me start from the beginning.

It was 1970 and a young European couple had been starting out their life together. Eric Bonde, a musician who played guitar in a band, twenty two years old, five feet six, clear blue eyes and light brown hair that shown a reddish tint in the sunlight. His twenty four years old wife Christina was a petite five feet four inches, with blue eyes and dark blond hair that she cut at shoulder length. They were expecting their second child and the delivery was near.

It was February 11th, 1970 at 1:13 p.m. when Christina delivered her beautiful baby girl. Unfortunately, the umbilical cord was wrapped around the baby's neck three times and the nurses had to rush the baby to the emergency room. When the scare was over and baby was doing well, they measured, weighed and completed the necessary steps before placing her tiny body gently upon her mother's chest. She only weighed 6 lbs, 9 ounces at 18.9 inches in length. The parents admired their daughter, a healthy baby girl with hardly any hair; only a whisper of light blond but curly hair, and her father's clear blue eyes. That baby girl was me, Hannah, and this is the story of my life.

My parents already had a three year old daughter, Annie who now had a baby sister. Annie was blond and had blue eyes just like me. My parents tell me that while my sister was a 'wild little girl', I was a very calm baby and that I just ate and slept, slept and ate. As I grew up, I was calm and easy going. All I needed was, as my mom would say, put me on the floor and I would play happily with my toys, until someone came to get me, minutes or hours later. I was a no-fuss baby.

At the age of five, I became interested in horses and my parents allowed both my sister and me to start taking riding lessons at a stable downtown Gothenburg. We advanced quickly and even though I was a short little girl, I had no fear of getting up on the big horses. Although I needed help to get on it, I definitely knew how to manage the horse once I was on it; an innate ability, I guess.

My favorite horse was Mackey, a little white and brown pony that I absolutely adored. I took lessons three days a week and sometimes more. There were days we spent all day just hanging out in the stables. We spoiled the horses, did our homework there, talked to people and helped the beginners who were just learning to ride. I loved it.

The people in my hometown have a saying that, 'quiet baby, rebel as a teenager'. I was. No, I wasn't! It was just circumstances;

circumstances that made me who I was. I would listen to advice, but went my own way, despite the advice. I was clearly independent.

When I started pre-school I had a smile on my face almost all the time and was easy to get along with, which made me popular with the other kids, even with my cousins and classmates.

My father was a businessman who traveled a lot while my mom stayed home with my sister and me. We were a happy family in my early years.

Things changed. My parents started to fight. When my dad came home from his trips, my parents would argue and disagree about everything. This resulted in my parents getting divorced. I was only six years old and it was hard on my sister and me not to have dad at home anymore.

Mom got full custody of us and kept the house my dad built. It was on the same property with my grandparents' house. Dad got a little one-bedroom apartment in the city, downtown Gothenburg. He was still working much, doing a lot of business out of town and out of the country. He also started to do business in our hometown and we treasured the time we could spend with our dad when he was home. He was always on the go and his mind occupied with his next business move, even when my sister and I were with him. He really never took the time to be just a father. To once in a while play or talk or listen to us. He didn't got involved in our interests as much as we so desperately needed at that time in our life.

Already in preschool it was very important for me to have my 'me time', although I loved to be around people. When I wanted to be alone, I would disappear for a few hours and when my mom became worried, she could always find me in our backyard, spending time by myself, talking to each and every flower in my grandmother's garden. They said I was a little dreamer. This, I would realize later in life, is what kept me alive and made me the strong woman that I am today.

MY PARENTS DIVORCED AND BOTH GOT REMARRIED

My sister Annie and I got accustomed to living with mom, without dad, and our lives became more peaceful, but only for a while.

The first year at school I was a happy, smiling chatterbox. I was always talking so it was easy for me to make new friends.

It wasn't quite a year after my parents' divorce when my father met Marilia, a very sophisticated looking Polish woman, who became his second wife. She didn't have any kids of her own and I don't think she really wanted any. Even at my young age, I got the feeling that Marilia never wanted to have anything to do with my sister and me, so we tried to stay out of her way as much as possible. She was distant, never warmed to us and just tolerated us because of our dad. And I know if she had to choose, we would never have been in the picture.

Anyhow, my mom Christina went out with her girlfriends a couple of times a month in the small city of Landvetter, where we lived. Mom met Conn, who became her boyfriend when he was only eighteen, and my mom was twenty-nine. When we first met this six foot, somewhat stocky Conn, I got the feeling he would never like me or my sister, he thought we were the 'bad' part of mom's family. The baggage he could do without. He liked to spend time with our mom but always shut us out, and we learned to entertain ourselves as best we could.

Conn never got involved with our activities until my father started to question my mom's choice of a boyfriend, and whether their relationship could bring anything good to our family when he was so young. My mother ignored dad's concerns and after a few months Conn moved in with us. Neither of us, Annie or me, was happy about it, but we were too young to be heard, or mom was just too selfish to care. I was seven and Annie was ten.

MY MOTHER'S NEW HUSBAND ABUSED HER

It was only within a few months after Conn moved in that they started to argue and of course, if there was alcohol involved it just made it worse. The quarrels were often a few times per month, but then it became more often even when there was no alcohol, he could always find a reason for an argument. I often heard them fighting at night, screaming at each other and my mom crying from time to time. I couldn't get any sleep. We saw her bruised and with a black eye but she stayed with him. I didn't understand. I remember one night he called our names, waking my sister and me up, and told us to come downstairs.

They were in the dining room. Annie and I looked down from upstairs and Conn had mom lying over his lap with her underwear down by her knees, he looked up at us and said,
"See what your mother is worth," . . .

while he spanked her with our dog's leash. We couldn't do anything to help and I felt her pain in my heart as tears fell down my cheeks. I didn't get any sleep that night. I prayed to God that Conn would stop abusing my mom and promised myself that I would never be with a man who abused me. Not mentally! Not physically!

I got in trouble at school the following day for the reason that I didn't get any sleep the night before. I couldn't keep my eyes open and my homework wasn't done correctly. My teacher pulled me aside and asked what was going on with me? I really didn't want to tell her for the simple reason that she was dating Conn's older brother, Dany.

Their fights would wake us up at night and they were becoming more frequently. I couldn't focus at school and my grades dropped. The school called my dad to get an explanation from him, but dad didn't know what was going on in our house, so the next time my sister and I went to see him, he sat us down and talked to us to try to figure it out.

We told him how much mom and Conn were fighting and how Conn had control over the whole house.

"Has he ever laid a hand on any of you?"

We told dad no, because he hadn't. He just didn't care for us at all.

Well, dad spoke to mom about leaving Conn, but she was a grown woman and made her own decisions and she chose to stay with Conn. The reality was hard for me to bear. We kids had a family with fighting, abuse, and no security or trust.

From time to time, I lived in my own mind, and my own world where everything was like a fairytale. To escape the truth I became more often the 'dreamer' and it made me strong. I promised myself that when I grew up, I would find my prince. We would get married, have kids and there would be only love, honesty, trust and respect between us. We would be there for each other, no matter what. We would live a normal life without drama, without fights, and I would never accept anyone who treated me badly.

I spent as much time as I could at my cousin Sofia's house or with my grandparents. It could be anywhere as long as I was away from home. I enjoyed Sofia's house, because it was so quiet; no fights, only laughter and warmth. Just like a home is supposed to be. I remember once we had a sleepover at Sofia's house where we stayed in her grandmother's little cottage. We sipped on cider and listened to music, danced and stayed up until early in the morning although we were just eight and nine years old. Good memories.

My cousin Sofia and I got along well, and we spent a lot of time together. We could be out all day long, walking around Sofia's neighborhood imagining what we would do when we got older; what kind of house we wanted and whom we were going to marry.

Once we came upon a little house that looked like it was abandoned and ready to fall apart. Something; curiosity perhaps, caused us to go in. We knew it wasn't right for us to enter someone else's property, but we did anyway. It was filthy and dusty with things tossed about all over the place, but we really liked the house. We found a broom and started to clean it up. We organized the things in the house and pretended it was our house. Before we realized it the time just flown by and it was getting dark, and time for us to go home. The house looked so cute to us, so we picked some flowers from the garden and put them in a cup of water, just in case someone lived there and came home there would be a surprise.

Sofia's mom was upset when we got home and asked where we had been all day and why we were coming home so late, when it was already dark. We told her what we had done and she became even more upset.

"Do you girls know what could have happened? The house could have fallen apart, or the people who own the house could have returned. What would you tell them?"

"Just that we thought it needed to be taken care of better."

Sofia's mom smiled at us and told us to get ready for bed so we did, and when we had turned off the light Sofia whispered,

"I think we were really nice and it looked so clean when we left."

"Yeah, I think so too," I answered quietly.
We fell asleep tired from cleaning all day.

One day my mother went to visit her friend Helene and she took me along with her. My mom's friend's son was Robert, a guy in the same grade as I that I hated.

"I'll never be friends with him," I told mom.

But no more than 15 minutes later Robert and I started to speak, we realized we liked a lot of the same things. We became the best of friends. Robert and I had made peace.

Everyone thought Robert and I had a crush on each other, but that wasn't the case, we were just best friends. He was eight and so was I. He took ballroom dancing lessons two days a week and I went to see him dance and that was my introduction to ballroom dancing. It looked like so much fun as I already loved to dance.

When I got home that night, I asked my mom if I could take dancing lessons too, and after talking to my dad they agreed that I could.

Robert and I became dancing partners but after a while Robert dropped out, but I continued. Every year at Rondo, we performed for our families and friends. We dressed up in such beautiful dresses and suites, just like princesses and princes. I couldn't wait for the yearly event, it was the highlight of the year and I even felt like a little princess.

OUR HOUSE BECAME MORE AND MORE A BROKEN HOME

Beginning the winter of 1978, my mom and Conn told us we were going to have another sibling. Mom was pregnant with Conn's baby. Conn had stopped beating her while she was pregnant and we prayed that he would mature and change now that he was going to have his own child. At the same time, my grandmother Molly, on my mother's side, became very ill. She had diabetes and now there was something wrong with her leg. We found out it was gangrene so serious and her leg had to be amputated from her knee down.

Grandma Molly died January 1979 and it was a big loss for me because she was my guardian, a strong woman with a heart filled with love for everyone. I used to go up to her every morning before I went to school and we would have coffee and home baked goodies together. I really looked up to her. Many times when I needed my mom, but she was too busy for me, Grandma Molly was the one who would comfort me.

Although my mom was selfish, she has always been very loving, but in a different way. She didn't think about how we were doing, or how we felt when she and Conn were fighting and Conn was abusing her. She didn't realize what damage it did to Annie and me.

Conn was sure the baby was a boy and when the delivery was near, he drew a big heart on my mother's belly and wrote with capital letters ED. That's the baby's name if it's a boy!

April 30th, it's a holiday when we celebrate the arrival of spring in Sweden, it was time. They left for the hospital and mom delivered a big, healthy baby boy. My brother was a big baby, both in height and weight, with blue eyes and just a few whispers of hair on his head. Conn got his wish, but we didn't. As soon as they came home with our brother, the abuse, both physical and mental, started up again even worse than before.

I had lots of friends and spent plenty of time with them, while my sister, Annie, had just started high school and didn't have too many friends. She stayed to herself and started to rebel. She dressed in camouflage clothes, dressed like a boy, colored her hair and was somewhat offensive towards everyone else.

Our parents were worried about Annie not having any interest in sports, school, friends, or boys, but she loved horses. To get her interested in something, dad bought her a horse when she turned thirteen and she started to spend all day at the stables with Doss, her horse. She stayed out with the other people who lived around the stables where she had Doss and she became friends with Klaus who had just moved to Landvetter from Gothenburg.

One day when I went to the stables to ride with Annie, this dark haired, cute guy stepped in and said hello to her.

"How do you know him Annie?"

"Oh, he is Klaus' younger brother, Pete."

I knew him from school and didn't like him at all because he was too flighty and somewhat 'hyper', and he had an attitude towards people he didn't knew. Although he was cute all of my classmates stayed away from him. Pete, who was in the same class as Robert, was known to be a real troublemaker. When I later started to talk to Pete, I realized he was a really nice guy and after that we became good friends and hung out at school.

When I was ten, I was having problems with my knee in gymnastics class at school. I asked my mom to write a note to allow me to skip the class but she did not believe me and thought I was lazy, so I had to continue with the gymnastics class and ignore the pain as much as I could. It got worse and the pain was more frequent, even outside of the gymnastics class. I now had pain while walking and after two months I started to limp. When my mother noticed the limp, she realized that I was telling the truth and that something was definitely wrong. She made an appointment to see the doctor. After examining the knee, and taking a series of x-rays, they still couldn't find anything wrong and we went back home. I didn't understand and it didn't matter what the doctor said; I was in pain and my knee was hurting.

The following day when I got home from school, my mom said that the doctor's office had called and that they had forgotten to take one x-ray and asked us to come back to have it done. This time they took an x-ray of my hip, and yes there was a problem. How serious it really was I wouldn't find out until later . . . . much later. Twenty-seven years later.

Most parents would ask questions and to find out what the problem was; why does she need surgery? How can we prevent the damage from getting worse etc. but the questions were not from my mom or dad. No questions to ask, less to remember.

When you are ten years old you trust your parents. It's not your responsibility to think of, find out or ask those kinds of questions. All I knew was that the doctor told my parents and me that they had to put a screw in my hip for some reason and it has to be there for a few years.

At that point, all I was worried and concerned about was if I would be able to go with my father and sister on vacation, but the doctor said that would be just fine. A few weeks later it was time for my surgery. It went very well and two weeks later, it was time for Annie, dad and me to start our vacation trip to Switzerland.

We traveled through Europe and crossed a few different countries, listened to music, laughed and of course my sister and I had a few fights in-between. I loved Switzerland and the people who worked at both the hotel and the little restaurant right next to the hotel where we stayed. My sister and I spent plenty of time playing games while our father had his business meetings.

When he spent time with us, we went out shopping, site seeing, and did other fun things like pedaling a boat on Lake Geneva, which was just outside our hotel. We went for walks and discovered the beautiful countryside. We drove to France over a weekend, but I really didn't like it there. The only thing that I enjoyed was when we went up to the Eiffel tower. We could only go to the second level because the top level was under construction. It was an awesome view from there, very beautiful, and everything looked so small from up there.

When we went out to dinner one night, I got the feeling that the people were mean, or maybe they just didn't like kids. I couldn't wait until it was time to go back to Switzerland, our hotel and all the friendly people. Overall, the whole trip was great and we bought our mother a very nice dress, which we would give her for her birthday when we got home.

We got back home and I had started school again, I met a new girl who started in my class and we got along pretty well, but I noticed she always wanted to be numero uno. We were opposites. She was tall and skinny and I was short and average. Our moms knew each other from work, so we became pretty close friends. I introduced her to Pete and they later became boyfriend and girlfriend.

Jean, another girl in our class that used to join us became friends with Pete's friend Daniel and I felt like the third wheel so I stopped seeing them as often after school. We simply grew apart.

Pete and I were still hanging out when we were with the horses and after two years my sister got tired of her horse, Doss, and got interested in guys instead. I ended up taking care of Doss and I loved him as if he were my own horse.

I spent all my free time at the stables; rode him, and brushed him until he was a shiny golden color. I would talk to him for hours and I loved him more than anyone can imagine. Annie decided to sell Doss and I was so sad but had nothing to say about it. After all, it was her horse.

A year later when I was 14, it was time to take the screw out of my hip and that meant another surgery. It wasn't a hard procedure and it went smoothly, but I was sore for a few weeks after. They cleaned the screw and gave it to me; to remind me of what I had been through. It was a big screw, about the size of a pen, five inches long and it looked like a big nail with a screw on the top. I couldn't believe it; I thought it was amazing that I had something that size in my hip.

MY FATHER OPEN SWEDEN'S FIRST STRIP CLUB

My dad was still married but had a mistress. Her name was Katina and she was a curvy, red haired woman with brown eyes. He gave her everything. An apartment downtown, a job, and he spent lots of time with her as well. My sister used to frequent the house and she often stayed with them.

Around the same time, my dad and his partner Bo opened a new business. It was Sweden's first strip club, which they named Maxxx. Soon after, they opened a second club and named it Dreamworld.

The whole city was talking about it and soon the talk reached our little town where my sister and I lived with our mom.

Some people thought it was okay and called it 'exotics dancing', while others thought it was absolutely unacceptable and nothing but prostitution. It was difficult not to be linked to the whole situation because we have a recognizable and unusual last name. It is dad's family name and he is well known, so when it was printed in the newspaper everyone knew it was our dad. The older children in our school started to call Annie and me 'the porno king's daughters' whenever they saw us. Even some adults started to look down on us when they saw any member of our family. I felt ashamed.

The clubs were going very well and they handled their business wisely. My dad made good money from it and soon after the opening, the police started to investigate, checking if everything was legal at both Maxxx and Dreamworld. They tried very hard to find a reason to shut the place down. The whole city was in an uproar with differing opinions about whether the clubs or the business was good or bad. My dad and Bo were smart businessmen and they stretched but didn't break the laws Sweden had about strip clubs. They were selling food but no alcohol; they kept the panties on and no touching, but still some people said it was the same as prostitution.

My dad, who has always liked nice things, bought a Rolls Royce so everyone knew it was him coming when he drove by. I was proud of my father in one way, but on the other hand, I didn't like the business he was in at all. When he would come to pick us up from school, I heard people commenting, talking and pointing at him, and I would wish he drove his wife's car instead or some other car.

Yes, it was nice to have a father who had money but at our age to be called names and with people trying to put you down and always having to defend ourselves and our family name, it was quite unpleasant. It was a very heavy burden and not worth it. Why couldn't I have a normal life?

MOTHER'S SECOND DIVORCE

When my brother was three years old he was going to tell my grandfather, who still lived on the same property where we lived, that the coffee was ready, but he came down and told my mom "Grandfather doesn't wake up mom," and she knew what it was before she saw him. The night before when he closed his eyes he went to be with the lord. He had been so unhappy since my grandmother past away three years before and now they were back together. Now another hit to us kids.

Conn and my mom decided to sell the house we grew up in, the house my dad built, to buy a townhouse downtown Landvetter so we could live closer to school, stores and buses. It would be more convenient they said. My sister and I did not want them to sell the house. We loved our house, but we had no influence at all in the matter.

We moved to the new townhouse and lived there for a short time, when Conn and mom decided to separate and divorce because they simply couldn't agree about anything. He was still abusing her and they were constantly fighting. I was happy about the divorce but it felt like I had already lost everything that was supposed to be my security—the trust in my parents and the house I grew up in. So from now on, I would only depend on myself.

My mom gave Conn full custody of Ed, because he didn't have any other kids and she had her two daughters. We moved out of the townhouse and into a two-bedroom apartment just a few blocks away from the townhouse. With a smaller place, my sister stayed most of the time with our dad's 'other woman,' Katina in her apartment. That meant Annie had the opportunity to spend more time with dad than I did.

Almost all the kids I went to preschool with were in the same class all the way through high school and one of my best friends from the start, was Peter. Peter was a slim, short boy and he was very friendly, just like I was. With his brown, always well-combed hair and a calm personality, he made me feel comfortable around him. Peter and I used to spend time together all the time during the first years and we used to be teased by the other kids who thought we were going to end up being boy friend and girl friend. But it wasn't like that between us and we were too young as well.

When we became interested in the opposite sex, we went our separate ways, and talked only at school or on the phone.
We still talked about everything and gave each other advice on relationships, and therefore he knew everything what was going on with me at the time. He was a great guy.

My sister started to be friendly with Lena, a new girl at school. Lena was two years older than I was, but somehow Lena and I had more in common with each other and became closer friends. Lena was new in our town and grew up in Kortedala, one town over from downtown Gothenburg. All her friends still lived there so we started to make that neighborhood our regular place on the weekends.

I was thirteen and had already started to smoke cigarettes and now when we were hanging out in Kortedala with her friends who were 18 or older, I started to drink alcohol as well and partied with them as often as we could.

At first, we used to interact only with them in Kortedala but after a while, we all took the tram or the bus to hang around downtown Gothenburg where there were many more people. In the summertime if the weather was nice, the avenue was the hot spot, but in the winter or when the weather was bad, we would stay in the mall, which was open 24 hours a day. The stores were closed but we could still be indoors. There was a diverse collection of people who were there at night; just about everyone. Young like me, homeless, alcoholics, people who smoked hash or those caught up on heavier drugs. There were all kinds of 'groups'; foreigners, people with varied beliefs, different colors and a many different tastes in music. A very varied collection of people.

Most of the time the different groups of people kept to themselves, but once in a while there would be a fight and someone would get killed.

If they had seen you before and you knew your way around the mall, it was cool, but if you looked lost, you could be in trouble. We got to know the regulars and became friends with them.

One weekend we had planned to party and I paid someone to buy a 24-count box of beer for Lena and me. I had hidden it under my bed at my mom's house. Conn came over and found it. He called my dad who came, took the beers and forced me to go with him. Why did he care now when he didn't seem to care otherwise or when I was doing well.

From now on, I was going to live with him he said, and I wasn't happy at all. I was so restless and bored in my dad's house as he was always caught up in business and hanging out with his friends. Even now when I lived with him, he still did not spend time with me. I wasn't allowed to either see or talk to my friends, but after only a week, I guess he got tired of me annoying him. He let me move back with my mom, and made me promise him that I would focus on school and stay away from the mall. It was too hard for me. All my friends were there. Everyone told me that my friends weren't good people, but they were all wrong. They never even took the time to try to get to know them, just time to judge my friends.

It was the stereotypical discussion that just because we hung out in the mall, we were all bad kids. I was the baby of our group of friends, and even though some of them smoked hash, and others did cocaine and some were into heavier drugs, they were always protective of me. They told me how bad it was for me, that I should look at them and see what damage the drugs had done to them, and damn that person if someone would try to give anything to me.

As all teenagers, I was curious and one time asked if I could have a try at smoking hash, but I was told a resounding "No! End of discussion!" That is how addiction starts, they told me, and I never asked again. It felt like they cared more for what happened to me, than my own parents did and I loved my friends.

Around the same time, my dad got a bigger apartment, a more spacious two-bedroom apartment in downtown Gothenburg, just a block from Dreamworld. First I loved to spend time there when my father was working and I could watch movies all night if I wanted to, all by myself. Even when I went out partying with my friends, there were times when I spent the night at his house instead of staying in the mall or sleeping at my friends' house in Kortedala. That was of course, if I could get in touch with him and if I was sober enough, or he was drunk enough, so he wouldn't notice that I'd been drinking.

MY FATHER'S GOOD FRIEND RAPED ME

One early morning, my dad came back home from all-night partying, he brought one of his 'good' friends home with him. His friend Jim was twenty-six, tall with short, blond hair and blue eyes. You could see he spent a lot of time in the gym. My father opened the door to my room to let me know that he was home and that he had one of his friends with him. I said, okay and went back to sleep.

My dad fell asleep on the couch because he was so drunk. I was sleeping but woke up to someone pulling up my blanket and getting into my bed. It was Jim. I was aghast! I pulled back on the covers and asked

"What are you doing?"

Instead of answering me, Jim put a finger over my lips and started to touch me all over my body. At the same time, he was telling me it's time for me to stop fooling around with these young guys and get a real man, just like him. I was still a virgin at that time. I had never slept with anyone and I told him I didn't want to and I was not going to sleep with him. I was still just a child, 13 years old!

"Time for you to become a woman. You're 13 years old, so just relax, he said."

"My dad is out there and he won't let you hurt me."

I felt secure and so sure my father would come and stop him and would never let anything happen to me at his own home, but Jim just smiled and said,

"What do you think your dad can do? He is way too drunk to do anything or to even help you. He's knocked out on the couch and won't hear you."

His voice was full of certainty and disdain as he started to get on top of me and when I started to scream, he put his hand over my mouth. Up until this point, I had the assurance; false assurance as it turned out, that he won't dare and I'm safe in my father's house. Now I felt the fear coming over me and I started to cry while I tried to squeeze my legs together to stop him from getting inside of me but it didn't help. He was too strong. He forced my legs apart, got in between them and I felt how he slowly pressed himself to get inside me.

I squeezed and tried to push him away from me, but he was so heavy and I couldn't move him. While he was raping me, I was hoping my dad would hear me. I was waiting and praying for my dad to come and rescue me. Dad never came, but Jim came inside me. Right after, he got out of the bed and looked at me.

"Don't you dare tell him, he won't believe you anyway. Who do you think he will believe?"

He had a smug smile on his face while he got dressed and left the room. After he left, I pulled the covers over my head. I was crying and wished I could have been far, far away from there.

I was panicking and tried to force my mind to go in to my dream mood. The fairytale world I lived in when I was younger to release myself from the pain I was feeling, but the thoughts in my head didn't want to leave me.

'What have I done to deserve this? What could I've done to stop him? What had I ever done to deserve something so painful and humiliating?'

These thoughts were going over and over in my head. I had an indescribable pain in my body. I felt something running down my inner thigh and when I looked down on my leg, I saw a kind of thickened light red stream going down my leg; it was blood mixed with his sperm. I felt sick! I thought I was going to faint. I felt like someone was trying to choke me. I couldn't breathe. My vagina, heart and soul, all of me hurt. I was abused! I felt so dirty, violated and worthless. I was just thirteen years old and had just been raped, in my father's house and by my father's friend!

Early the next morning before my dad woke up, I left the house and caught the bus back to my mom's house. I felt so ashamed, so dirty and promised myself never to tell anyone about it.

I was just going to erase the night from my memory and move on with my life, but I was sure of one thing; I would never again spend the night at my dad's house if he had friends over.

My mom was surprised to see me but she didn't ask why I came home so early in the morning, and I just said hi and got in the shower. I did my best to scrub every bit of evidence of him from me, every fingerprint from my body, but I still felt dirty when I was done.

I have always been a girl who believed that I can have, and that I'm worth the fairy tale, but now because of this disgrace, I was sure I could never get it. I was too dirty and not worthy of true love. I did my best and was successful not to tell anyone. I just kept quiet and went on with my life. One day when my sister and I were on the bus to downtown she asked if I wanted to go to our dad's house? but I told her,

"No" . . .

"Why Hannah, you never want to go there these days."

"Yeah I know, but it's not fun over there."

"You didn't feel like that before, did something happen?"

"Kind of"... I replied.

"So tell me..."

"I will tell you only if you promise not to tell anyone, not even mom or dad."

"Sure I promise," she said, and I told her what had happen that night.

She let me finish and when I was done she said that I had to tell our dad, but I replied.

"No I can't. He is not going to believe me because Jim is his friend."

And that's how the conversation on that subject ended.

School was not going well for me and I was tired of all the schoolwork I had to do mostly by myself without any help or encouragement from anyone. I was exhausted from always being strong and trying to keep my head up. There were times I just wanted to break down and cry; just to let myself fall, but I knew there was no one there to catch me.

Lena had moved back to Kortedala so we just saw each other occasionally now. My self-confidence was very low and I started to gain weight. I wasn't a big girl but I thought I was bigger than the other girls in my class, and I felt like an outsider and that I wasn't good enough. I withdrew from my classmates more and more and was becoming depressed and introverted.

In seventh grade, a girl named Monica was in the classroom next to mine. She was a taller and bigger girl than me, but her self-confidence was high. I silently admired her for the way she carried herself and for the confidence she had.

One day we started to talk and I realized that she was a very sweet girl. We connected right away and in time, we became the best of friends. Her family was so nice and they treated me as if I was a family member; another daughter. I had a crush on her older brother Tom, while she had a crush on his friend Lars, whom I knew from the stables where Doss, my sister's horse used to be. Lars lived next to the stables. We hung out in their house all the time and fantasized about how much fun it would be if all four of us got together. I think the guys knew we had a crush on them from the beginning. I spent a lot of time there, it was almost as if I had moved in with them. Everyone knew that if you saw one of us, the other one was not far behind. No one could separate us.

One day when I slept at my mom's house, she told me that my dad would be coming over and they wanted to talk to me.

"About what?"

She said they would let me know when dad got there and once he arrived, we sat down in the living room and I looked at my dad and then my mom.

"Hannah, I want you to tell me what happened in my apartment when Jim was there."

I thought I was going to die. They knew because Annie had told them even though she promised me she wouldn't. I was trying to make light of it and mumbled

"Nothing,"

but of course they didn't believe me. So I told them how Jim came into my bedroom as soon as my dad fell asleep and raped me, how he disrespected both me and my dad.

"Why didn't you tell me this earlier Hannah, and why didn't you call me when I was there?"

"And why didn't you come and help me, dad? I was calling out for you dad. I did! I was waiting for you to come and make him stop, but you had been drinking. You were asleep and didn't hear me dad."

Tears were running down my cheeks now.

"Would you have believed me even though he is your friend?"

"Yes, of course I would, and no he is not a friend! A friend wouldn't do anything like that."

That was all he said and after that, the subject was dropped.

I didn't sleep well at all that night and in the morning when I went to school I couldn't focus. When they brought the issue up last night, they woke up all that pain I have been hiding and now that it came up again I felt completely worthless and not lovable at all.

I TRY TO TAKE MY LIFE AT 13 YEARS OF AGE

In 1983, Monica and I were going to hook up as usual at our lunch break, but I changed my plans and went home instead. I knew no one would be there at that time and I needed some time to myself. I was exhausted from trying to act as if all was well. I had no strength left to keep pretending that it was and that I was healthy. I felt as if my whole life was a bad soap opera, and I was the main character while faking a smile and pretending to be happy. All I wanted was to have a normal life. 'Was that too much to ask?' I said out loud.

I thought about what my future could be like and how I could make it happen. The truth cut like a knife in my heart. I cannot pretend any more. I have no strength left. I am alive but it feels like I am dead or dying. I might as well finish it.

These thoughts crossed my mind, but how would I do it? I don't want it to hurt. If I cut my wrists and it doesn't work, that will hurt. I could take some pills and just slowly fall asleep. That's an option. That's the option I thought and walked into my mother's bedroom.

'There must be some pills around here somewhere. There has to be.'

I looked where my mother would keep them. "Sleeping pills. Made sense to keep them close to her bed," I said talking to myself as I opened her nightstand drawer. Here they are! I hesitated only a few seconds before I reached for them and had them in my hand. This will help me get over the pain. I was surprisingly calm. Back in my room, I opened the container and counted the pills to make sure I had what I thought was enough to take my life; there were some 70 or so pills. I swallowed them all, a few at the time until the container was empty, and then I lay down on my bed. I couldn't wait for them to release me from all the hurt, pain and sorrow. I had carried all these emotions inside me, in my soul, in my body, locked away in my mind for much too long. I don't know if it was the pills but I felt so relaxed, or was it because I knew that in a short while I would finally be free.

Suddenly I heard the phone ring, but it was far, far away so I didn't have to answer. After the phone had been ringing for while, I thought to myself, *'why doesn't someone answer the phone?'* and then, *'whoever it is will get tired and hang up,'* but the phone kept on ringing and ringing. I couldn't stand the buzzing, or the tone, whatever. I crawled out of bed, picked up the phone and with a groggy, sleepy, drugged up voice said,

"Hello."
"Where are you and what are you doing girl?"

It took a second or two for me to connect with what was being said,

"What?" but then I understood and continued, "Oh, I'm home and not feeling very well, I'm about to go to sleep."

It was Monica. She abruptly hung up on me and a few minutes later, still sitting on the floor with the phone in my hand, Monica was banging on my door.

"Open the door Hannah! I know you're in there!"

Why would she show up right now? Knock, knock, knock again. This time more determined than before.

'*Damn just leave me alone Monica,*' but I knew she wasn't going anywhere without talking to me.

"If you don't open the door before I count to three, I'm calling the police. I'm serious Hannah."

I pulled myself up from the floor and took the few steps and opened the door. Monica looked at me. My eyes were glassy and my speech slurred and incoherent.

"What are you doing here Monica? You are supposed to be in class."

"So are you."

Monica pushed pass me and hurried to my room. I stumbled after her, crashed down on the bed and put my head in my hands.

"What have you been doing baby girl?"

Monica asked as she sat down and put her arm around my shoulders and held me. I could feel her heart beating, and she gently moved away some of my hair from my face. Monica was so caring and sweet and I know she'll be sad when I'm gone. I also know that with the passage of time, she'll be okay. She would find another best friend. I tried to be strong, but when I looked up and my eyes met hers, I couldn't hold back the helplessness in my voice and I said,

"I can't do this anymore Monica, I just can't. It hurts too much and I'm too tired."

Monica knew something was terribly wrong and had never seen me weak like this before.

"Hannah you know I love you and you've got to tell me what you did, what's happening to you."

I didn't want to tell her so I just sat there quiet.

"Hannah you've got to . . ." but as Monica turned her head to look at me, she saw the empty container on the nightstand. She didn't even finish the sentence as she put the pieces of the scene together and figured out my problem.

"Why Hannah? You should've talked to me. That's what friends are for and you know how much I love you."

My vision was blurry and I started to doze off, and didn't respond very well when Monica was talking to me. She pulled me up on my feet and out in the hallway where the phone was while hugging and stroking me the whole time as she whispered in my ear.

"Don't leave me Hannah, I need you."

She dialed the number to the school nurse and asked for help. The nurse came to my house and with Monica's help they both managed to get me in the backseat of the nurse's car and she took me to the hospital's Emergency Room while Monica had to go back to school. At the ER, the doctor saw me immediately and not knowing what kind of pills I had taken, they had to induce vomiting as soon as they could by putting a tube down my throat. It was disgusting and I believe that was the last time I vomited.

A nurse then put me in a room and told me to rest until my parents got here.

"Please don't call them. It's not necessary and my parents are too busy anyway. It's not that important."

I think, by regulation, parents need to be notified of critical situations like mine if the child is under 18 years old, so the nurse had no choice but to call them.

Mom and dad both arrived at the hospital, but the way they behaved, I wished they had never been called to the hospital. Mom's eyes were red from crying and my dad's eyes were red from drinking the night before. When we were alone in a room, waiting for a psychologist, my father asked me,

"What kind of serious problems do you really have Hannah, to do something so stupid and drastic?"

When I didn't answered him, my father continued,

"Make me look like a fool . . ."

I was right about my parents and wanted to shout "what about me, and how I feel, my feelings?!" Instead, I chose not to respond to my father's question even though I had an answer, but the answer wouldn't be good enough for them. My parents would never understand me, or my precarious situation.

It was all about how I felt and the heavy burden I had been carrying alone for so many years. My parents had never listened to me before, so why would I think they would listen now. Why even try to explain. I sat there, rubbing my hands together to try to stop them from shaking, but I remained quiet.

Then we talked to the therapist, her name was Dr. Jonsson. When she asked what problems we had in our family, neither of my parents said anything—no problem, no issue. Dr. Jonsson looked at me,

"It has to be something when you try to commit suicide at thirteen."

Her voice was soft, sweet and comforting, but I didn't feel comfortable and secure enough to talk about it. It wouldn't matter anyway when everyone else was not addressing the problem.

I was sad and wasn't really thinking of the consequences, I tried to convince myself. Dr. Jonsson then just let us leave. As we walked out to the cars my father grabbed my arm. I felt his fingers around my wrist, and felt the blood pulsing in my veins; I was ready to start defending myself again. My father blamed me for being selfish. I had ruined his day by dragging him down to the ER for something so stupid. For nothing!

Nothing I do is good enough for him. *'I am damned if I do and damned if I don't,'* I thought to myself.

We went separate ways. I was going home with my mother to get some rest as I was emotionally exhausted after this ordeal and didn't want to talk to anyone.
The next time I went to Monica's house, her parents asked me to sit down because they wanted to talk to me. I felt the warmth from Monica's mother as she caressed my hair and said,

"Hannah, Monica told us what happened and we are so sorry. Remember that we are always here for you. If you feel like you need to get away from home for a while, you're always welcome to stay with us for however long you want. You're like a second daughter to us."

"Thank you so much," I said. "Even if I would want to, I don't think my parents would let me."

I was right!

MAY 1985 WHEN I FIRST MET JARED

I had just turned 15 years old when I met this handsome young guy. It was one of those times when we hung out at the mall downtown Gothenburg. I was running to catch the bus when, bang! I just cut the corner and ran right into this six-foot, blond guy. I was just about to tell him to watch where he was going, when I looked up and into the most beautiful eyes I had ever seen. I got a tingle through my body. My cheeks flushed red from blushing and all I could do was post a shy smile and say,

"Hi."

We struck up a conversation. His name was Jared. Of course, I missed the bus, but there would be another one soon enough.
Jared said he had seen me at the mall before and wanted to talk to me, but I was always surrounded by other people. He seemed nice and after talking for an hour or so, it was time for me to say goodbye as I had promised my mom that I would not to be late. As I turned to walk away, I turned and looked at Jared,

"I see you around, huh?"

"Count on it. Can I have your phone number?"

"Sure, I said."

We exchanged phone numbers and Jared called me that same night just to 'make sure I got home safely,' he said and I thought that was cute.

Jared lived with his mom in Frolunda, on the other side of the city and would be seventeen in October. That meant Jared was two years older than I was. After that meeting, we talked on the phone almost every evening and approximately a week or so later, I started thinking that Jared really liked me, but I kept my distance. He always gave me compliments, called every day and always asked what I had been doing during the day. I thought he was very caring, but I would find out the real deal soon enough.

A few weeks later, when I saw him I gave him a hug and then pulled him aside and asked,

"So you want me to be your girlfriend?"

"Yeah, I'd love that," as he took my hand in his.

"Let's go for it. If it works fine, but if not, there is nothing lost."

I guess Jared was very, very pleased because of the way he looked at me and the firm, warm hug he gave me. It held so much promise but wasn't a big deal for me. I mean, I liked him but only time would tell if it would work out. If I had had the slightest idea of what was coming, I would not have made that suggestion, of my being his girlfriend.

My relationship with Jared started in May 1985, I was in the 8th grade and in the beginning everything was wonderful. Life was great and I had a cute blond boyfriend with hazel brown eyes. We saw each other as much as possible and had sleepovers almost every night in my house or his. When we had been together for about a month, we had sex for the first time.

Two months went by and one day when we were at his mom's house, just talking and snuggled on the bed in his room, Jared asked me about Peter and why we were such good friends.

"We've known each other since preschool and been best friends since then. We enjoy each other's company."

"Oh, okay, but from now on, Peter won't be your friend any more, right?"

"Peter is my friend forever," I replied with a big smile.

Jared didn't like that answer I gave to him.

Bang! he punched me right in the face. I had the taste of blood in my mouth and lost my vision for a second. My cheek pulsed and I felt the rush of blood to my cheek. His action surprised me because I had never seen him like that before. I couldn't believe what had happened. No one had ever hit me before. Not my parents or anyone, so I was shocked and confused. When I looked at him, Jared's eyes were darker than normal, almost black and he looked somewhat 'crazy'.

"Why did you do something like that?"

I said while rubbing my cheek, which was hurting badly.

"You just told me that you're choosing him over me. How do you expect me to react? I don't like the way you talk about him, to him or any other guys for that matter. I guess someone has to teach you how to talk and act."

I wasn't used to anyone telling me what to do, and I had heard enough so I got up and started to walk towards the door.

"I am leaving now. I don't want to be here anymore." I said.

Jared jumps up, locks me in and pushes me to the floor.

"You're not going anywhere. I'm not done with you," he said.

When he raised his hand to hit me again, I screamed, and just then his mom, Eileen, knocked at the door.

"Is everything ok in there? What's going on?"

Jared answered nicely;

"Everything is fine, just a little accident."

He looked at me with his finger over his mouth, warning me to be silent. After his mother moved away from the door, Jared told me with a voice I didn't recognize,

"It doesn't matter if you leave me, because you're mine anyway. You're going to give me what I want and when I want it, you are mine forever. It doesn't matter if you have another boyfriend, you'll never get rid of me!"

The look in his eyes, told me it was more than a threat, it was a promise!

Before I left his house to go home that night, Jared told me how sad he was and promised it would never happen again. That was the first time Jared laid his hands on me, but definitely not the last.

I couldn't stop thinking about it on the way home, and I was still in shock when I got home but pushed it to the back of my mind. When I asked myself why Jared was acting like that, I found myself making all these excuses for him; maybe he was just having a very bad day and reacted before thinking. I didn't do anything wrong so there must be some kind of excuse for him to act that way. Right? I didn't call Jared that night when I got home as I usually do, but he called me in the morning.

"Hey darling, did you sleep well?"

"Not really, but it was ok."

"How come?"

"Because I kept thinking about what you did yesterday and I have been searching for some kind of an explanation as to why you did it."

"What did I do?" Jared said.

"When you hit me."

"I didn't hit you."

"What?!"

I couldn't believe what he said.

"Jared you know you did."

He kept denying it, so I just said 'whatever' and dropped it. He was regretting his action, I thought, and he didn't want to talk about it. At least that was my thinking at the time.

It should have been a warning for me but you know the saying, *Love is blind.*
It was only a week after and Jared hit me a second time, and again without provocation. I began to see more and more of Jared's controlling behavior of his own household, which included his mother and younger sister.

What I found contradictory was, Jared was practicing karate and had been doing so since he was 14 years old. He had already achieved a Yellow Belt and should have known and acquired the discipline taught in such coursework. Karate is only to be used for self-defense and the karate teachers teach their students discipline, and insist that they fully understand the discipline. I also know that Jared had strong respect for his master. That's why I could not understand how he could simply ignore what he had been taught. For Jared, there was always a reason to fight, with everything and everyone, but, of course, it was always someone else's fault. We missed a bus because he stayed in the shower too long. It was my fault because I should have told him to hurry up.

Once when I told him to hurry, he beat me up because I was causing him stress. Another time it was because he couldn't find a paper; a paper he himself had placed under some other papers. Jared also got physical if I didn't want to have sex when he woke me up at 4:00 a.m., when I was tired, or had to get up in two hours to go to school.

That first year close to our summer break, Jared asked if I wanted to go to Finland with him for four weeks to visit his family and his father who was in prison. We would take a train across the country, starting south all the way up north, but I said,

"No, not for four weeks. That is too long."

"Can you think about it before you give me an answer?"

"No, I don't want to leave for that long, and we really don't know each other that well yet."

We had not been together that long and I also wanted to hang out with my friends during the summer. To go shopping, hang by the beach if the weather allowed, and just catch up and enjoy life. I didn't want be alone with him, in a country I was not familiar with and knew no one, with him and his erratic behavior. Jared got discouraged, but he asked me again a few days later,

"How about we compromise Hannah? If I shorten the trip and just go for only two weeks, will you come with me?"

"Let me think about it, Jared. I'll talk it over with my mother and if it's okay with her . . ." I said and yes, mom said I could go for two weeks.

Jared was so happy when I told him and only a week later his mother accompanied us to the train station.

"Did you tell your mother you'll be gone for four weeks Hannah?"

"No, we are only going for two weeks Eileen!"

She turns her head towards Jared and so did I. Jared looked kind of surprised at first but managed to quickly recover and said,

"Oh nothing."

He grabbed my hand with one hand and the bags with the other. He said goodbye to his mother and we got on the train. When we were seated and the train started to exit the station, I asked again.

"What did your mother mean Jared? You told her we were leaving for only two weeks, right?"

"Hannah, the trip is four weeks, but the only way to make you change your mind and come with me, was to say we are going for a shorter time. You were very determined not to go for a whole month!"

I got upset because I didn't want to be gone for that long and now it was too late for me to turn back, so I thought, 'okay Hannah, just make the best of it. It cannot be that much of a difference,' but I still didn't like the fact that Jared lied to me so easily. That should have been one of many red flags, but oh well!

We visited with his family on his father's side and stayed for a few days. I couldn't speak any Finnish, but Jared could and some of his family could speak and understand a little Swedish, so communicating was not a problem. His family lived out there in the middle of nowhere on a dirt road and his uncles let us borrow a car so we could get around, even though neither of us had a driver's license.

That first evening we all had dinner together, and Jared who always spoke to me in a terse tone if I didn't do what pleased him, was on his best behavior and did quite well. But the second evening, because I told him that he should get what he wanted to drink, because I was eating, he became quarrelsome. He smiled as he turned his head towards me, but his eyes became extremely dark.

"Hannah," he said in Swedish, "do what I tell you to do, or we'll have a nice little chat when we get back to our room."

One of his aunts responded, "Jared if you're thirsty, don't be lazy. Go and get something to drink, it's in the fridge." Jared got up, but the look he gave me told me he wasn't happy about what had happened. I kept thinking to myself, *'what did I do?'* At this point, I was still used to speaking my mind and having my own opinion without anyone 'correcting' me. I always had an open mind, was happy and easy going, and almost never put myself in harm's way, and I knew the difference between right and wrong. Jared's reaction was really bothering me. *We would talk and straighten it out later tonight,'* I thought. *'Jared don't know me well enough yet to know my personality.'* I brought it up when we got to our room that night but Jared just said,

"Hey Hannah, we're at my family's house and it's my rules. Okay? Don't be so fucking sluggish, just do what I'm telling you and we'll have a wonderful vacation."

"But what if I don't want to Jared, you can't force me. I thought we were going to enjoy this summer and each other. Not argue and fight."

"We won't argue Hannah; as long as you do what I tell you."

I shook my head, thinking, *'this is crazy,'* but I was totally in his hands. Jared was the one who knew the surroundings and the people around here. His family seemed to like me and they treated me kindly.

A few days later we continued our trip. We visited his father in prison (my first time visiting a prison), and we stopped at the home of Eileen's good friends, Erkki and his wife. They were very nice and friendly. They told us how Erkki had visited Eileen when Jared was a baby and other fun memories. We had a great time while in their company, but as soon as we were alone, Jared decided what to do, when to do it and how to do it. Everything.

He would decide everything from when we would go for a walk to when we were going to have sex. Whether I was in the mood or not, for one reason or another, but when Jared said it was time, it was time. I had to do his bidding and if I didn't, it was a reason for him to start a fight.

When we were on our way back home and again passed by his father's family house, Jared asked if we could try anal sex.

"No! That is disgusting Jared.'

"You don't know until you try it, so let us do it," Jared said and wanted me to turn over on my stomach.

I had that old feeling when my stomach tensed up and I got scared. I tried to find a way out.

"No, I'm not doing it Jared. I'm serious."

"Son of a bitch!" Jared said and twisted my arm so I rolled over on my stomach and as soon as I was in that position, he laid down on top of me. My heart started beating faster and my mouth got dry. Suddenly it was *déjà vu* and it was two years prior and back at my dad's house.

Same situation, different men! I did not want this, but there is nothing I could do. I was helpless.

With all of his body weight on me, I couldn't move and he kept forcing himself into me. Again, I squeezed my legs and buttocks together as hard as I could trying to resist and for him to realize it wouldn't work. He knew I was doing my best to stop him, so he forced his hands under my hips, dug his fingernails into my pubic bone. It really hurt so my automatic reaction was to pull up to stop the pain. That gave him the in he wanted, he pushed hard and he was in.

With his hand over my mouth I couldn't scream, although I tried, but there wouldn't be anyone there to help me. I just waited for him to finish and forced myself to think of something else, just to forget the pain as I was hurting badly.

"It wasn't that bad honey, right? You should be happy; it felt so good for me."

Jared was satisfied and that was all that matter to him!

"Take a shower, you are bleeding."

I was more than happy to get away from him, even for just a few minutes. Once I turned on the water and stepped in the shower, I started to cry. I sat down on the floor and just let it all come out. I was so hurt and insulted, and felt so helpless.

Once again I was raped, this time by my own boyfriend. I just wanted to go home, but we had a few more days before we finally would be home. I didn't sleep much that night.

Come morning, Jared was the charming, 'normal' guy again. Everyone just adored him when he seemed normal like this, and I thought,' *why can't he always be like this?* When he was the controlling person, his eyes turned black and he became the devil himself.

We arrived home and Eileen asked how the trip was?

"It was okay. The country was very nice, with all the little lakes, trees and forest. One of the most beautiful countries I've seen."

Eileen knew that her son was abusing me, along with her and his sisters. So not to make it worse I kept all the answers short. Then Jared wanted me to stay at his mother's house that night. I told him, "Not tonight."

I told him my friends and parents; 'they want to see me now. I have been gone for a whole month.'

I didn't tell my mother what had happened; just told her to tell him I wasn't home. I didn't want to give him a chance to have control over my mind again. Two days later Jared was standing outside my mother's door waiting for me when I got home.

"Hannah, why are you avoiding me? If I have I done anything to make you upset, talk to me baby!"

"Anything? I don't want to, and I'm not going to do this anymore Jared. When I talk, you don't listen to what I'm saying. Just let me move on with my life and you can go on with yours and be happy with another girl."

"I'll never let you go and I don't want another girl, end of discussion!"

"I'm not doing this anymore Jared. That's it! Stop playing games. Okay?"

He took a step closer to me and put his hands behind my neck while he pulled me closer, looking directly into my eyes.

"Hannah, when are you going to realize, the game is not over until I say so! We can do this the easy way, or the hard way, but whatever choice you make, it's *my way!* Either you play with me, or against me, the choice is yours!"

I stayed with him, I didn't know how to get rid of him, and I still didn't have the strength to get out from it all by myself. I hoped that my parents, and especially my mother, who had been abused by her second husband, would take charge and save me from this situation. Force me out of it; send me to a border school or whatever. I was only fifteen years old, but my parents didn't do anything. Once again, both my father and my mother were too busy with their own life to react to the control Jared had over me and see how bad he was treating me.

There was always an excuse for him to beat me up, always! From then on, my life started to go downhill, and fast.

I was losing myself and my psychological outlook was bleak. I didn't say what was on my mind anymore, because I was really too scared of him. I was still in high school and after all the abuse I was living in fear.

I told Peter about it and told him how scared I was of Jared, and how he said he'd never let me go. Peter told me I did not have to live in fear and didn't have to live scared.

"What can he do? Jared won't do anything around your mother in her house when you're there. When you're at school, I'm there."

That was so sweet and it gave me some strength, at least until I spoke to Jared by phone and told him that I want it to be over.

"Over?" Jared laughed, "no way Hannah. I will never let you go and do you really think someone can protect you from me?" Jared continue, "Is the little boy Peter going to be your white knight and fight me or what? You know Peter wouldn't have a chance. Do you really believe when it comes down to it, that he would risk his life for you?
You're mine until the day I die Hannah, or until you die. End of discussion! I'll see you later love, okay?"

He hung up the phone.

Jared was right. Peter would not have a chance against him, and I would never put Peter, or anyone else for that matter, at risk for me and my problems. When the weekend came and Jared asked what time I was coming over, I said I would be there by 8:00 p.m. I could hear the smile in his voice when he said,

"Good girl."

Once again Jared had exercised his power, the control he had over me. When I explained to Peter, he refused to understand. It was difficult for people to really understand. How could I make him understand when Peter hadn't seen that side of Jared. Some of my friends knew Jared wasn't nice to me, and that Jared could be aggressive, but they had never seen his evil side and could not possibly understand why I was so scared of him and even more fearful to leave him.

Jared had two sisters, Pauli and Marla. Pauli was nineteen and had her own apartment in the same complex as their mom, and Marla was twelve and still living with her mom and Jared. Their parents had divorced when Jared was four and that was when their dad moved back to Finland.

There were days we enjoyed without fight or argument. Those days Jared could be so sweet and lovable and I was sure he loved me and would stop beating me up some day. I just have to give him time and prove to him that he is the only person I loved and didn't care for any other guy.

It was rare that a whole week passed without a beating. I always found some reason to excuse him when he hit me even though I knew it was wrong; he was stressed, his allergies made him like that, or maybe I shouldn't have said anything, or he was tired. I could go on and on, that's how blind and brainwashed I was.

That's not really true, the truth is I lied to myself and I wished it were different, but the real reason I had for not leaving at that point, was fear. I was scared to death of what Jared would do to me and no one understood; or maybe they closed their eyes and refused to see how dangerous the situation actually was.

I kept on seeing Jared and as time passed, I became genuinely good friends with his sisters, especially Marla at that time. Pauli was engaged to Ron, and they were expecting their first baby in October that year. Marla and I on the other hand, talked and did girly stuff together; we went shopping for clothes, and would play around with hair and makeup. However, when Jared got mad at either of us, we tried to protect each other as best we could.

I know all families argue and siblings fight occasionally because I did in my family, but Jared was the one in charge here. Most of the time when he got mad at someone, he was out of control in a way that wasn't normal. He would throw things. He would bang or throw chairs onto the wall, kick the walls so hard causing big holes in the walls. He broke anything that was in his way.

On the other hand, there were times when there would be no throwing, no banging or kicking on things, but at those times he would beat on us instead. Not only Marla and me, but also his own mother. We would all be screaming, one louder than the other, and there were times when if his mother, Eileen got a chance to get away, she would call the police. Jared would grab me and pull me along to run out and catch the bus to my mom's house so he wouldn't be arrested.

He also warned us that if the police ever put him in jail because either of us, his mom or me, called them . . . . he didn't finish the sentence.

"Remember, even if the police take me in, I will eventually get out, dearie."

That sentence is forever branded in my memory.

Of the four of us, I was the one who could control my temper best and would stay calm, but every time Jared hit Marla or his mother, I feared it made him grow stronger. It hurt because I couldn't do anything to help them or to make him stop. I was, and felt very powerless. Jared didn't listen to anyone and at times when I tried to help by telling him to stop or tried to pull him away from them, he punched me too and would say

"Oh, you want some too, huh?"

Once when Pauli was over visiting her mother, Jared started to argue with her about something. She was pregnant at the time, and Jared threatened to kick her in her stomach. Pauli got upset and of course she told her fiancée Ron. Ron had a talk with Jared the next time he saw him, and told Jared that if he so much as laid a finger on Pauli, he would be a dead man. Jared had respect for Ron and knew that he was a much stronger man, but it was different with us females. We didn't have the strength to fight back.

When we were at my mother's house and mom was home, or when we were around our friends, Jared didn't touch me even if I said something he didn't like. He solely gave me the look; *just wait until we are alone* . . . and he made sure I got the message. None of this behavior surfaced in the first month. Therefore, I had no idea what would happen next.

It was my last year in high school, and I was tired of school, mentally and emotionally. I just wanted to get a job and make some money so we could get our own apartment. Maybe getting away from all the other stresses his mother put him through at times; again, my excuses for his behavior, as usual. Maybe that would help him to calm down. I spent a lot of time at his house and it was a hassle for me to get to and from school as I had to take the bus. It seemed to work well in the beginning, I suppose because it was new, but it became a hassle. We always stayed up late watching TV, or we were fighting with each other or his family. This resulted in my losing sleep. I would only get a few hours sleep before it was time to get up and be off to school.

The nights when I got to bed on time, Jared woke me up in the middle of the night for one reason or another. I didn't have time to be with my friends anymore because Jared and I always spent so much time together. For the reason that of this erratic schedule, I started to skip school. First only once in a while, but when Jared dropped out from college, it became more and more often. There were times when I wanted to go to school, but Jared didn't let me go.

"You might go and fuck someone else," he would attack me with wounding words.

Jared didn't have a clue that that was the farthest thing from my mind. I hadn't even given something like that a fleeting thought. Other times I couldn't go because I had a black eye or I was simply too tired emotionally to focus.

My teacher, Mr. Larsson, talked to me a few times about my falling grades, but I think even he had given up on me by then. It didn't matter what either Mr. Larsson or my parents said anyway. If my parents had tried harder, putting more effort into getting me to go to school, I am sure I would have gone. While my parents knew where I was and what was going on in my relationship, Mr. Larsson just thought I was tired of school. When I had only two months of high school left, I stopped going to school all together. My grades were already so bad. My only passing grades were in English, Swedish, math and handicraft, (cooking or creative crafts). There was no way for me to get my other grades up before graduation, so I stayed home.

I had planned not to attend the graduation, but two days before I told Jared that I actually wanted to go. He looked distrusting at me, but said okay. I got so emotional and started to cry. These are people I've known since I was a little girl and now it's time to go our separate ways. It was time for all of us to enter the adult world and make choices as to what direction to take. We might never see each other again.

I told my mother I was going, and it was time to figure out what to wear. We didn't have any money and when I asked my mother, she said she was broke. I had no time to get any cash from my father and had to make the best of what we had. I tried on one of my mother's dresses, a white summery dress and the shoes I picked had a small heel. The result was nice and I picked some flowers to add some color to my outfit.

Friday and graduation day was here! I was very pleased with how I looked that day, and for once, I was on time. When I walked in the door at school, I realized how much I had missed it and now it was too late for me to catch up. *'Oh well, there is nothing I can do to correct it now.'* I probably had this feeling because I knew I was not coming back. I opened the door to my classroom and just about everyone was there. It got quiet when I walked in but Peter's eyes lit up and he was the first one to jump up from his chair and came over to give me a hug.

"Hannah, I've missed you," he whispered in my ear when he put his arms around me. It was very emotional and made me sobbing.

"I missed you too."

"Is everything okay Hannah?"

I looked down at the floor, so he wouldn't see the sorrow in my eyes.

"Let's not talk about it today Peter, today is a happy day. Remember how long we've been waiting for this moment?" I said and gave him a big smile.

I only had a short time to catch up with my classmates for a minute before I heard someone saying,

"Is this really you Hannah?" It was our teacher.

"Yes it's me."

"I didn't think you were going to show up. Come on this is the day we've been waiting on forever!"

I looked at him and laughed.

"I'm so happy you're here Hannah, and I wish you all the best in life. You're a great girl."

"Thank you," I responded.

I gave him a big hug before it was time to go out where all the other classes were and it was time to graduate. When the day was over, I was so happy I had attended.

It was 1986, I started to work part time, and Jared was also working, but he couldn't keep a job for one reason or another. At best, he kept a job for a few months and then he either got tired of the job and quit, or he got fired. We were fighting as much as ever, or even more now that I was out of school and we had more time together. I didn't want anyone to find out Jared was beating me, but they saw me bruised and black eyed, but didn't ask me anything. My parents knew, but didn't do anything. I felt ashamed. I was embarrassed, especially in front of my friends and co-workers.

From time to time, it was hard for me to keep a job because of the embarrassment or showing up to work all black and blue and bruised. I would call in sick, or I spend hours putting make up on, trying to cover up the bruises. I was becoming more and more a loner and not by choice. Even my closest friends kept their distance from me. I am sure they suspected something was wrong, but I didn't tell anyone about it and they didn't ask.

At the beginning of our relationship, Jared had been around some of my friends, but shortly thereafter, he would frequently lose his temper either with me or with my friends. They would often tell me that having to ask permission to visit friends or go shopping was such bullshit! That I shouldn't be putting up with things like that, so because of the uneasy and often unnerving situations, they would invite me out, but not Jared. Of course, I was being the good girlfriend and stood in defense of my boyfriend, even though I knew Jared was wrong and that he indeed acted like a jerk.

Again, my friends would tell me that I didn't need people like Jared in my life and he was not good for me, that he had a bad influence on me, and that I deserved someone better. Then Jared would tell me that my friends were jealous because I had a boyfriend. That would place me in the middle, between him and my friends. I decided to choose and the choice would make me lonelier than ever, but I was sure my friends would understand my choice if they knew the truth. I never told them. I didn't want them to dislike him even more or think that I was weak or stupid for staying with him.

I thought my friends really wouldn't understand how evil and dangerous Jared could be, so I let them believe I was the bad one and a bad friend. In my head and in my heart, I had decided to spare them and not have him in their life.

So once again, I had to sacrifice and experience the hurt and pain of being the victim of an abusive man. I wasn't just a victim of abuse, it was also the loneliness, the emotional, physical and mental pain which forced me to trust no one but myself. I had no support from my parents or other family members, and because of my silence, my friends didn't know because I never gave them the chance to find out. Why should my friends help me when my own family didn't? The people who loved me, either walked away from me or I had to turn my back on them. I didn't want to jeopardize their safety.

Jared and I, both started working, cleaning cruise ships while they were in dock. One day while working I met Lizbeth, a girl whose name I had heard about from Jared, but I didn't know who she was, so I asked her if she knew Jared.

"No I don't," she said, "but he did ask me out to dinner once."

Tears filled my eyes and I went looking for him and found him in the lobby. Jared looked at me and asked

"What's wrong Ha . . . . ?"

Before he finished the sentence, I slapped him in the face and walked away without saying a word; the girl was right behind me so he figured it out. I was quite angry and hurt and I didn't want to even speak to him on the bus ride back home.

Jared knew he was the one doing something wrong, but now he tried to cover it up and blame it on me. He tried speaking to me but I didn't answer. So, in typical fashion, Jared went into his usual rage.

"If you ever touch me like that again Hannah . . ."

"So what would happen then?" I asked. "Are you going to beat me up? As you always do?"

"Do it one more time and you'll see what happens."

I shocked myself and couldn't believe I had slapped him, but it was the one and only time I had ever hit him. He kept flirting with other girls whether I was there or not, and comparing me with his ex-girlfriends. He would often say, she did this or she did that. I always gave him the same response.

"So she did, but I'm not her, Jared. I am *me!*"

On the other hand, when Jared was in his good mood, he was sweet towards me and would say things like; 'no one could ever take my place in his heart.'

My Father and Marilia decided to get a divorce and my dad bought a condo in London. Now he was traveling back and forth a whole lot between London and Sweden. My dad and his partner had some disagreements about the businesses, and decided to go their separate ways. Bo, dad's partner, took Maxxx and my father got Dreamworld.

My father also started another business. It was a combination of a little grocery store, video rental and diner, which stayed open 24-7 and he named it *Always Awake*. It was convenient for my dad as he had *Dreamworld* on the third floor and *Always Awake* on the first floor of the same building.

Between these two businesses and traveling, my dad soon realized he needed help taking care of one thing or another. My sister became the manager for *Dreamworld*, handling everything from opening to closing, shopping and hiring strippers. My father started to date Liza, a 23-year-old woman who worked at a casino as a dealer at one of Gothenburg's hotels and was the cousin of a waitress at *Always Awake*. She had a 6-year-old daughter named Pamela. Liza would stop by after work to see her cousin and that is how they met.

The relationship became more serious and her family started to travel with my dad when he went out of town. All the responsibility at Dreamworld was now on my sister, and as the distance between Annie and me got bigger and bigger, we didn't have much in common. When I met Jared and introduced him to Annie, the bad vibe was already noticeable.

Annie hired two young women, Mya and Cathy who had recently moved from Stockholm to Gothenburg. Both of them had been in a gentleman's magazine, and Annie became friendly with them and started to spend time with them outside of work.

I had heard gossip at *Always Awake* where both my old friend Monica and I worked on the weekends. Annie didn't like to be around people and especially not pretty girls and it was also one of *Dreamworld's* policies, not to socialize with the employees. I got a uncomfortable feeling when I first met Mya and Cathy because I had heard that they were doing loads of drugs.

I knew my dad had a zero-tolerance drug policy with his business and his employees. One of his policies when hiring strippers was, they should have no issues with alcohol and absolutely no involvement with any kind of drugs. A few months later, I found out that Annie was doing drugs as well. That really surprised me. Annie was doing cocaine but when I found out, it was hard for me to believe. My sister never drank alcohol or smoked cigarettes, but went straight to cocaine! It was really hard to believe that was Annie. Since I was the black sheep in my family and I smoked cigarettes and drank alcohol, when I told my parents about Annie, they didn't believe me.

My friend Monica asked what was going on with me? She said I was not myself anymore, and she was worried about me. They thought I lied about Annie to put myself in a better light. I felt it was so unfair but left it up to my parents to handle it the way they thought best. Dad eventually got the proof he needed, and found out that I was telling the truth and went up to *Dreamworld* to clean it up. He fired Mya, Cathy and several others.

It is now 1990 and my father bought a little house in Marbella, Spain, for himself and Liza. He told Annie to come visit with them for a few weeks and she gladly did. Dad had decided to move to Spain, permanently, so he came back to Sweden for a few months to wrap up some business. He gave Annie his new Volvo 760 Turbo, and told Annie she could move in to his apartment, but it was still in his name and he paid for it of course. Before dad went back to Spain, he gave Annie some money so she could cover everyday expenses.

I never understood that and I didn't think it was wise, because as soon as dad left, Annie bought drugs and got high with her friends—people who knew she had money. That was the reason most of the people hung out with Annie—they knew she got money from dad or she stole it from *Dreamworld*.

I had never been to Spain or London because I wanted Jared to come with me, but because my father and Jared didn't really like each other, Jared was not allowed to come. For one of my dad's birthdays, he rented a yacht in Monte Carlo and invited everyone in the family. Dad flew them in from Spain, Yugoslavia and Italy (where Liza and her family are from) and Sweden. Since I wasn't allowed to bring Jared, I declined the invitation. Jared and I had been together for three years by then, so I thought it was a serious relationship, not just a fling. Because I stand up for what I believe in, it wasn't a hard decision to decline the invitation even though I really wanted to go. But it was both of us, or none of us!

Jared would put me through hell if I decided to leave without him. I kept thinking that sooner or later my father would have to accept Jared. He was my boyfriend and would be my husband one day, so I had decided that if my father wanted me in his life, he would have to include Jared too.

With one person or another trying to tell me what to do, made me more determined not to listen to anyone. However, Jared still had the last word in every matter! Deep inside I knew the reason my father didn't like Jared, was because of the abuse he was well aware of. My parents didn't do anything to get me away from him when I was still under age, and they didn't do anything before Jared had this hold over me.

They thought I was only being stubborn. I seemed to do what made my life easier, and more important, I was doing what was needed to stay alive. I kept telling myself it was because even though Jared was a jerk, he was my jerk. I had convinced myself or was somewhat sure that Jared just needed to grow up and be a man; and then he would start treating me better because I was sure he loved me.

My sister who was a "yes daddy or no daddy" girl to just about everything dad said, went to Monte Carlo and as always, came back with a stack of money. She had been taking care of Dreamworld for a few years and from time to time, she went to visit dad, in either Spain or London. When she came back, she always had a lot of money and it was "party time". *Dreamworld* was losing money and dad finally told Annie to have his friend Harry take over the business.

She could still keep the apartment and car because dad paid all the bills so she didn't have to look for another job. She could just relax and get high as often as she wanted.

Then Annie met Freddie, a handsome Yugoslavian and they started dating. I never knew whether it was for the money or the drugs, or if Freddie actually liked her, but they dated for a few years. Freddie was also a drug addict although he didn't look like one.

To fill some sort of a void or to have something to do and care for, Annie bought a Germany shepherd puppy, and named him Rambo. He was the calmest of dogs and loved everyone, especially Jared and Freddie. Unfortunately, Jared was allergic to animals, so even I had to stay away from them as much as possible so Jared didn't get an allergic attack. When he had an attack, his mood was horrifying and of course, I got blamed.

Once when Annie went to Spain to visit dad, Freddie took care of Rambo as he did many times before but this time it was different. When my sister came home, she noticed something had happened to Rambo. He wasn't the happy, friendly dog he used to be before she left for Spain, he was now scared of people. My sister's neighbor told her that one day they had heard Freddie beating the dog. Rambo was crying so badly, they couldn't stand it and they had to call the police. Even though my sister and I didn't talk often, this really hurt and made both Jared and me angry. Annie called the police to see what truly happened and what the police told her was insane.

When the police arrived at the apartment Freddie first refused to open the door, but after a while he let them in. Rambo was lying on the floor and didn't respond when the police called his name. They asked Freddie what happened to the dog? He told them that the Rambo didn't listen to him so he had to let the dog know who was the boss. There wasn't any proof of abuse and it was 'just' a dog, so the officers left again.

'JUST a dog, just an animal! What kind of nonsense is that? Rambo can't talk to tell what happened so there was no crime, nothing they could've done.' It made me so angry to hear that, and behind my anger was also my own situation. There was nothing the police could do for the animal, and there is nothing the police could do for me. There is no one who can protect me. Poor Rambo, he must have been so scared. There is no guarantee you will come out of abusive situations alive. Swedish laws suck's! Honestly!

We could see Rambo was in pain and my sister took him to the vet. The vet said Rambo had some internal damage but nothing they could do about it. He was never the same and Rambo passed away a few weeks after the incident.

Dad and Jared had started to talk to each other a little more. This made me happy and hopeful for a better future with family bonding on both sides. I wanted our children, when it was time, to grow up in a big family, knowing as many relatives as possible. Even though I lived a life filled with physical and mental abuse, I still had hope for a great future and did my best to see the good in everyone. I was still dreaming for my life to be a fairy tale, my fairy tale. Once again, just like I did as a little girl, I escaped the tough life I was living and got lost in my dream-world.

My father had always been obsessed with, and thought women should be skinny, but neither Annie nor I was slim. I was now 17 and gaining weight, which I in one way appreciated; it got my attention off from the opposite sex.

After spending only a few months with Jared, it was better and safer for me and others, if I didn't get the attention. Jared would attack and beat a guy just for looking at me. This, of course, made me feel guilty even though I knew it wasn't my fault, but the fact is; if I was not there, it would not had happen. Jared had me so under his power and control that from time to time, I even felt guilty that I was alive.

My stress level was incredible high and my monthly cycle stopped. I kept gaining weight, and my self-esteem plummeted. It didn't help when Jared would use aspects of my family life to put me down even more. He would often mention that my father was a porno king or my mother a weak alcoholic, and my sister was a crack head. He often would say that I was fat and stupid and that no one would ever love me and that I couldn't do anything right. He also would remind me quite often that I even got raped in my father's house. No one could ever love me so I should be happy and thankful to him for being in my life. That is how it was when Jared was upset about something.

When everything was okay between us, Jared declared how much he loved and needed me and what a good woman I was. At times like that he would ask,

"What would I do without you Hannah?"

I always gave him the same answer.

"Find someone else."

The reason I felt like that, was because there was no security in the relationship and no respect, because wherever Jared went, he would flirt with other girls. Many times he would hit on a girl right in front of me.

I remember once a girl passed by us and Jared turned around to look at her, and his remark was,

"That girl is one sexy ass."

His hair was long at the time, so I grabbed it and pulled as hard as I could. Hearing him say that and in front of me, made me feel like I got stabbed in the chest. He never said anything like that to me.

I, of course, didn't think of the consequences at that very moment, but Jared pinched my arm and that was enough for me to know I had crossed the line. When we got home, Jared smacked me with his fist right in the face, which resulted in bloody nose and the day after, I had two black eyes and a big bruise on my arm. My mother saw me one of the following evenings, but she didn't say a word, didn't ask about my very visible black eyes, no mention of anything having to do with my appearance at all.

MY DESIRE TO START A FAMILY OF OUR OWN

That same year, still under all that nervous tension, my monthly cycle had still not returned after it had been regular and monthly for the previous five years. I was not concerned at first, but this went on for almost a year. Then Jared and I started to talk about wanting kids, so I went to the doctor to see what was wrong. I consulted with a reputable doctor and he administered tests but said there was nothing wrong and we would just have to wait and see. Being around his sister Pauli and her family, by now they had two boys, Jay who was two and half, and Tim was a new born, made my longing to have kids and start a family of our own stronger.

I was 18 years old, but Jared and I had been together for three years and we got engaged May 3, 1988. Jared didn't propose to me, it was more that we decided it was time and bought our rings. It is different in Sweden, when you get engaged and married, both parties get rings.

I was sure we were going to be together forever and even if our relationship was like a roller coaster and Jared was extremely controlling and beat me up, I was sure he loved me and that my love would cure and change him.

He had so much other pressure in his life but I thought that if I just stayed quiet and didn't put more stress on him, he would stop the abuse. It put a lot more stress on me but at the time it was better me than him, I could handle the stress better, but it was just another bad excuse I made for him.

I had heard about couples who badly wanted kids but couldn't conceive for one reason or another, and that it would sometimes take years. I thought if we started now we would have many years ahead of us, we wouldn't be anxious because of our age. Time was passing by, and the more I was around children the more I wanted my own, but we had plenty of time and there was no need to rush things.

Jared had constantly told me that I wasn't a smart girl and when I thought of my grades from school, I didn't know if I was smart enough to get pass the reading part of the exam at traffic school to get my driver's license. It worried me but when I took the test, I only had three mistakes. I was in fact surprised when I got my test results, as the Swedish written test is very difficult and some questions tricky.

When I did the driving test, I didn't pass the first time out, but made it the second time and got my driver's license. I was so happy and felt independent. We rented a car and went to the restaurant where my father, who was visiting from Spain, always hung out with his friends, to tell him the big news. The whole gang was there having dinner and my father was sitting at the end of the table as always. I went over to him, gave him a big hug and kiss, and whispered in his ear

"I got my driver's license today dad."

I looked him straight in his eyes to see his reaction, to see if I got his approval. Dad knew I'd paid for it all by myself and both driving lessons and the tests cost a lot of money. He gave me a huge broad smile as he squeezed both my hands, before he gave me another hug.

"Congratulations, sweetheart."

"Thanks dad," I replied and saw in his eyes how proud he was of me at that moment.

It felt great to get my father's approval for once. We were going up to the Avenue to have a drink after dinner and I asked dad if he wanted to ride with me.

"Of course, Hannah, I wouldn't want to go with anyone else."

That was one of the only times when I felt and saw how proud my dad was of me and we had a great evening.

It is now 1988 and I was working in a factory located in Molnlycke, I had bought my own 1980 SAAB 900 Turbo and I was so cheery. I wasn't as lucky as my sister who got her car from dad, but as always I found my own way to get what I needed.

Now at eighteen I had got my driver's license, had bought my own car with my own money without help from my parents. My sister also had her own car, but everything that Annie had, dad had bought her. For me this was a very special moment where I showed I could take care of myself.

Another year went by and my period still had not returned. It worried me and we went to Sahlgrenska hospital where I took more intensive tests to find out what the problem was, and what we should do about the issue. The doctor asked me numerous questions including if I used birth control but I told him no, we wanted children. He said one possibility I didn't have my period could be because I was over-weight. Birth control would make it easier to lose weight he continued, and would regulate the cycle so that I would know exactly when my period would come. At the time I weighed 160 lb and he suggested that maybe I should try to lose some weight. It was almost impossible for me, even though I didn't eat much, I just didn't lose any weight.

We tried various options and when nothing worked, we; the doctor, Jared and me discussed and decided to try in vitro fertilization (IFV). That meant several hospital visits for months, but if it worked, it would definitely be worth it. The hospital accepted our application for IVF, and we were very happy. I was sure it would work and started to daydream about it—*'when we have a baby, I would have someone I could love unconditionally, and who would love me unconditionally. I'm going to be a mom.'*

The procedure started with shutting down my hormones by giving me shots every day. When the tests showed the hormones were low enough, the doctor built them back up under strict observation by giving me a different shot twice a day. After a week or so, the nurses started to draw blood to monitor my hormone levels and after another 5-10 days, they started ultrasound tests to see when my eggs were ready to be inseminated with Jared's sperm. This meant we had to go there at least once every day; sometimes even twice a day. I was the one getting the shots but Jared went with me most time as it involved both of us and I was happy for the support. During these times, it gave me hope and belief that Jared would eventually stop the abuse and stop beating me. I thought that if we had a child he would be more mature and have a different responsibility and focus.

The procedure required at least 4-5 mature eggs and when it was time, we both went to the hospital in the morning and the atmosphere in the car were nervous and tense. My doctor was Dr. Lenny, the best doctor, who was going to harvest the eggs, and he made me feel calm. The procedure went very well and Dr. Lenny harvested 7 eggs, 5 of which were fertilized and the cells grew well enough in a few days to be implanted.

When it was time to insert the eggs, Dr. Lenny decided to implant only two eggs, as they looked promising. Also, by Swedish laws, they were not allowed to implant more than three at the time. The other three were frozen in case the implanted eggs were rejected and now all we could do was to wait and pray, pray and wait.

The nurses gave me estrogen every day to give the eggs a better chance at success. Just the possibility of being pregnant with my own baby, put a smile on my face and warmed in my whole body. I know what a great mother I would be and that my child would never be without love and someone to care for him/her, someone he/she could always count on. I was flooded with so many feelings it was confusing, but finally it would be someone who loved me unconditionally. I have so much love to give, but no one who allowed me to love him/her.

The following two weeks felt like the longest in my life and every day, all day, I was praying the procedure would be successful. Sixteen days after the eggs were implanted, my period came and I felt the pain and emptiness of loss. I can't really describe it. I cried all day, was depressed for weeks and the emptiness I felt in my heart was indescribable. There was nothing that could take away the sorrow I felt, and nothing that could fill that empty space in my heart.

Life must go on, so I pulled myself together and focused on everything and anything else to help distract me. I got the usual wishes of sympathy from people who tried to comfort me and told me that it was all right; better luck next time, it's not too late, it's your first try and I know how you feel. None of that helped. If you have never been through this, you cannot know how it feels. It was a hard hit for Jared and me but it was easier for Jared to get over it. He didn't feel the physical side effects from the procedure, the emotional effects of the hormones, the bruises.

Instead Jared would bring it up when we argued and would say,

> "You are not even a real woman! Real women get pregnant and you can't. Why is that? Are you purposely doing something not to get pregnant or what?"

How could he say and ask me something like that when he knew damn well how much I wanted a child. Those words made me feel even worse about the situation and about myself. Time heals everything and it did, but it also left a deep scare in my soul. There was good news though, frozen eggs usually 'drop cells', but ours had been growing. So when it was time for our second try, we didn't have to go through the full procedure. We only had to do the hormone once, but again, we didn't have any luck.

I could not understand why when our eggs and everything looked so great. Why is it that I couldn't get pregnant? We tried this procedure a total of five times; three times we had to go through the whole process, and twice we had frozen eggs; still no success. We did our best on keeping the faith after each failure, but my hope died little by little, and it started to hurt more and more. This happened over a period of years as we had to take a break between attempts to let my body heal, and give myself a chance to get head and emotions together. The scar just became bigger and bigger, the sorrow in my soul deepened, but I kept on fighting to stay strong. Maybe it's just not meant to be for us to be parents, I thought, but honestly I couldn't believe that.

I love kids and at least I had the pleasure to be around and 'spoil' my two nephews with much love.

In September 1991, Pauli and Ron had another baby boy, Nick. We teased them and asked if they didn't know how to make girls? Now they had three adorable boys, and even though I missed having my own baby, I couldn't be happier for them.

In 1989 Jared and I decided to buy a condo. We wanted our own space, but we could not afford a house in Gothenburg. We found a condo an hour away from the city and after the bank approved me for a loan, we bought it but it was a huge mistake. I think we bought the house just to have something, rather than really wanting it. It was something *we* had control over but the bottom line is that it was just another impulsive investment on which we ended up losing a lot of money. Everyone told us that we would be too far from our job and friends, but we ignored them. We said that it would be fine, that we didn't mind driving and even though I hesitated, Jared was very convincing that it would be fine. Still we spent many nights in either his or my mother's house for one reason or another; the condo needed a lot of work, we didn't have any furniture, and we had no money. Also, when it was time for Jared to go into the military, he didn't want me driving that distance by myself.

While Jared was in the military, I had a break in my everyday stress dealing with him and I had a chance to take care of myself. He was stationed in Boras where he spent some nights, but other times I picked him up and he stayed with me at my mother's house, only to return to the base early the following morning.

Soon after we had bought the condo in Uddevalla, I realized it was a big mistake. It took way too much time for us to go back and forth, so we rented an apartment in Gothenburg, which left us with two rents every month and I was stressing myself out even more. I begged Jared for us to sell the condo, but Jared said, before we even start to think about selling, we had to fix it up, paint it, put tile in the bathroom and hardwood floor in the other rooms. We already had some of the material but no money to pay someone to fix it because Jared is not very handy or patient to do things like that himself. So now we had mortgage on the condo, rent for the apartment, a car payment and miscellaneous other bills, and because Jared had always messed up priorities we couldn't pay our bills. We were behind at least one month's rent on each place and I tried to convince Jared that we needed to calculate, to make a budget and manage our money better.

He had all these great ideas how we could get money but first we had to spend money. We rented a truck and in the middle of the night, went to this place where they collected pledge bottles and recycled tins, packed trash bag after trash bag until the whole truck was packed. Thereafter we drove straight to the Brewery in the morning to drop them off and get paid. Then we would go back home, take a shower and Jared took me to work, before he went home to get his rest. No wonder I was tired and had such a hard time focusing.

Jared and I had different priorities and at one point the bank threatened they would sell the condo. Jared was furious and told me I had to come up with some way so we would not lose all that money he had put into the condo. I found an excuse and bought ourselves a little extension of time. Meanwhile Jared got a hold of Safen, a guy he had known for a long time, and who had fixed his mother's apartment years ago and had done a good job. Safen put in the hardwood floors and the tile in the bathroom, and we slowly got the condo repaired and looking nice. I just wanted to get rid of it but Jared was sure we would make money on it if we just took our time. I knew we could if we had the money to pay the mortgage, but at this point, I had the bank breathing down my neck and no more wiggle room. To make a long story short, I ended up losing the condo and still owed the bank almost as much as I borrowed.

I was in deep debt and it was all in my name. Jared's credit was bad and he had not been working and didn't have a steady source of income. We tried, or more accurately, I did my best to manage our money in a way so we could meet our obligations, but with Jared making other priorities and 'investments' as he called them, which he claimed would make our money grow but of course never did, put us deeper in debt. There was no way I could keep up with our bills and many times we didn't even have money for food or our rent for months.

After constant worry over money on top of all the other stress Jared put me through, a couple of years later I asked my father for help. Dad said he would think about it and shortly after asked me for all the information about my debt and said he would see what he could do. He helped and covered some of the debts for me so I at least didn't owe the bank for the car or the condo, but my credit was totally messed up and now Jared was acting even worse.

After a few months even Harry was having problems managing Dreamworld, and when my father found out through Jared and me, that Harry was dating Maria, one of the strippers, my father fired them both. To my surprise, my father asked Jared to help him get his business back on track and Jared gladly accepted the offer. My father would let Jared manage his strip club but there was one condition, I was not allowed to be there, no excuses and no exemptions. Jared said he would comply with dad's request while I thought it was unfair, dad had let Annie manage it for a few years and now I was not allowed to be there. I didn't realize then that dad was trying to protect me, but the one I truly needed protection from was Jared.

In the beginning I stayed away, but after only a few weeks it was so unorganized and too much for Jared to handle by himself. I was more organized and knew how to get the business back on the right track, so we both started working together, off the record, of course. All the girls who worked there, knew I was the owner's daughter and unlike my sister, the girls respected me. Jared and I had ideas how it should be managed and how we would get the club successful again. When we put our heads together and worked as a team, the business started to turn around.

Around the same time, my father and Liza found out that several things were missing from their apartment, where Annie lived; things worth approximately $10,000 and my father suspected Annie or some of her friends had sold them to get money so they could buy drugs. Dad and Liza told Annie that she had to move out of the apartment. This was convenient for Jared and me because we didn't have any place to live, so we moved in and traded places.

There was a big difference between my sister and me; I had never done any drugs. I handled my business and had a smart head on my shoulders. I was smoking cigarettes and was drinking alcohol occasionally, but that was it. I was of the same thought as my dad regarding drugs and stayed away from that stuff. I've seen what damage it can do to people and I thank God for my friends who in my early teenage years had been so protective of me. It was thanks to them and my strong personality that kept me alive and out of trouble during those years.

I know that some times, or most of the times, you have to spend money to make even more money, so we invested some of the money from dad's business. We put some ads in the paper when it was payday; we cleaned up the place and gave it a better reputation than it had before. Jared was all excited but I had lived with him long enough to know that he always got carried away, and I did my best to convince him to think before we did anything. We worked long hours and after a while, it was hard to get Jared to wake up to go to work and open on time and/or shop for inventory. That made us run out of beer, sodas and other things that actually made money for the business. When I suggested some solutions we could do to make it work better, Jared didn't listen to me, he was the boss.

Sometimes when I couldn't get him to wake up and he didn't let me go over and open by myself, the girls said there were customers who would've spent money but we were not open, so the customers left. Besides that, if we had a customer who didn't know how to act or if the girls had trouble with someone, instead of calling the police, Jared took care of it himself and sometimes he went too far and the girls got scared. I told him to stop doing things like that, that he would be the only one who ended up in trouble, but again, why listen to me?

My sister was angry and jealous because dad let us stay at his apartment, and gave us the responsibility of managing the club. I think that it was at this point when things really got sour between my sister Annie and me.

Jared woke me up as soon as he came home this particular morning, which was not unusual, although I had hoped that he would let me sleep.

"Where did you put the car Hannah when you got home last night?"

"In the parking lot, why?"

"Because I'm asking you, that's why."

"If you look out the living room window, it's right there cross the street. I am tired Jared, please let me sleep."

Jared went to the living room and looked out the window and came right back.

"Hannah, the car is not there. Are you sure you parked it there?" he asked while looking out the other windows as well.

"Yes I did."

Now I was wide awake. I got up and looked out and he was right, there was no car.

"It's been stolen Jared," I said and I felt the anxiety coming over me.

"What the fuck, did you forget to lock it or what?"

"Of course I locked the car."

"If you weren't going home before me, this would never have happened Hannah. Why do you always have to be such a crybaby?" and continued copying me, "I'm tired can I go home. Am I stupid, letting someone steal our car, eh?"

"You know it's not like that."

"I don't know a shit Hannah."

Now, not only do I have to deal with my car being stolen, but I also have to deal with his bullshit. I called the police and told them what happened and the officer said I had to come in to file a report. I got dressed and we took the tram down to the police station where we filed the report. Then we went back home and I was just about to call my insurance company when the police called me.

"Did you find my car?" I asked all excited.

"Yes we did, but your car is not stolen Hannah."

"What do you mean, it's not stolen?"

"Your car got towed because your car was on fire. Someone set your car on fire where you parked it. Do you have any idea who would do that?"

"Hold up! Are you telling me my car was on fire? How bad is it?"

"It's totally burned out Hannah. Do you have any idea who could've done this?"

"No sir, I have no clue."

I was totally confused. *'What my car on fire? Who would have, could have done something like that?'* When I hang up from the police, I told Jared what had happened. I already knew what was coming from him, and yes, of course, it was my fault too. I figured no more sleep for me and while we were going back and forth about who could have done this, we looked at each other and I shook my head.

"No Jared, my sister could not possibly have set my car on fire, she would not, would she?"

"Yeah, that crack head can do whatever, so don't try to protect her."

"Oh my God! It is her!"

We were always arguing and fighting with her. I love my sister but she is so destroyed from all the drugs. Annie has been doing drugs for a lot of years, and it has always been that we were in competition about everything. More often than not, I got what I wanted myself and my sister got what she wanted from dad. Although, upon reflection, I am grateful that my father didn't spoil me, because that way, it taught me responsibility and made me very determined to figure out how to get the things I want by myself. At the time being young and immature, it did hurt me and I asked my mother quite a few times if she was sure my father really was my father.

I called Annie up and confronted her, but of course, she acted surprised. My sister denied it and told me to "fuck off", but I didn't expect anything different from her. I already knew. I wanted to go and see how badly the damage of my car was, so we went to the closest gas station, rented a car and drove to the impound lot where my car was; or should I say, what was left of my car. I almost cried, it was totally burned out. Only the skeleton remained, nothing else. My first car that I bought after I had gotten my driver's license, all by myself, and it wasn't even paid off yet. My own sister did this to me. What a shame! It was a hassle with my insurance company who thought we had done the damage ourselves to get insurance money from them and after the back and forth hassle, they sent me a check to replace my car. In spite of everything it wasn't enough, I still owed the bank $3,000.

The business was like a roller coaster and so was the income. My father started to question Jared's way of managing Dreamworld, And why he never got any money from the club. Jared told him how he needed some time to get it on top again, but as we made some advance there would be a setback, it was one step forward, the other step back.

After about six months with nothing but bad results, my father closed Dreamworld.

When Marla, Jared's younger sister grew up and started high school, we somehow grew apart. But while I was doing almost everything with her brother, and just like their mother, put up with his attitude, bullshit, abuse, while trying to encourage him to be responsible and mature, I didn't talk back to him to keep "the peace" in the family, Marla talked back. From time to time she fought with him and most of those times it was like a war zone in that house when we were there, as both Jared and Marla have hot tempers. Many times Jared ended up shutting Marla down, either by beating her up or she gave up and left the house. Other times Marla or her mother would call the police which resulted in Jared and I had to take off again, as so many times before, so the police wouldn't catch him and take him to jail.

Marla was out partying with her friends, or she hung out with me, and she started to date. We had some real fun memories together Marla and I; some of her first 'adventures' were with me. I'm easy going and not particularly material, so I let her spread her wings and try new things. A young, maturing girl had to start somewhere and I knew right from wrong. I would never let her down or encourage her to do anything erroneous—maybe a little wild and crazy, but not anything that was bad for her.

Some of the things we did together—the first time Marla drove a car; it was with me and with our car. She had a minor accident and dented the car but we hid that from her brother because I knew Jared would be furious and not only at me, but at her too. When Marla did her first party evening on the Danish cruise ship; that was with me. Marla and I would spend time alone, without Jared, and we got along so well and always had a blast together.

In 1990, Jared started a new job and met Tommy whose parents were also from Finland. They became good friends and a few times the foursome, Jared and I and Tommy and Marla would hang out, and after a short while Marla and Tommy fell in love. Marla and Tommy got an apartment together and even though she was only 16 years old and still in school but with Tommy's support, they pulled it off.

One evening in early 1991, the four of us had dinner when Marla told us she was pregnant. Although she was only 17, they decided they were going to have the baby. Marla was going to finish college anyway and she had the support of her mother and Tommy's parents.

I was very happy for them, but it cut me like a knife in the heart when I heard. All kinds of thoughts went through my head, I couldn't help it. It was not fair. They had only been together for a few months and they were going to have a baby. Jared and I had been together for five years and I never got pregnant. And we tried! I had to stop myself right there as our difficulty to get pregnant, had nothing to do with Marla and Tommy. It wasn't their fault and it wasn't fair of me to be envious or jealous.

A few months into her pregnancy, the doctor discovered some complications as Marla's blood pressure was extremely high and with further medical checks they found the problem. They wanted to keep her in the hospital for further observation but Marla declined. She said she would keep the appointments and as often as the doctors wanted her to, but she was not willing to stay in the hospital. On June 11, 1991, Tommy called to say Marla had delivered a baby girl.

"What? The baby is not due until August!"

"I know but the doctor had to do a C-section last night. The baby was in danger. Marla started to take blood from the baby instead of the other way around."

"So how is the baby doing?"

"She's very tiny, but she is okay."

Tommy and Marla had a room but the doctor had the baby under observation to see how she was doing on her own.

That same afternoon, Jared and I went up to the hospital and the baby was so cute, but oh so little. No wonder, she was born two months earlier than she was due.

Marla and Tommy named their little daughter Nessa and thank God, everything turned out just fine with her. The sad part was that early 1992, Tommy and Marla decided to break up and go their separate ways. It was hard for them to stay friends and make decisions and agree about their daughter.

While all this was going on and because we knew Tommy as well, Jared and Marla were fighting from time to time and once again, it ended up with me in the middle. Marla was one of my best friends, but Jared was my fiancé, and Marla often took the position that even if I hadn't done anything wrong, and it was Jared's fault, I was at fault too.

Marla and Pauli, Jared's sisters, had an argument and stopped all contact with each other. Not too long after this, Marla stopped talking to Jared and me. She told their mother Eileen, not to discuss anything about her, Marla, or Baby Nessa with us. That cut off all communication and contact with them, but sometimes when Eileen babysat her granddaughter, we had a chance to see and spend some time with her. Nessa was growing up to be a very demanding little girl but she was irresistible. She adored me and could sit in my lap forever; she would just snuggle and play with my long painted fingernails. Nessa was calm when I was around and other times there was no end to her energy. This link stopped when Marla found out and she told her mother that if she let us see Nessa one more time without her knowledge, Eileen wouldn't be able to see Baby Nessa again.

I missed both of them because the bottom line was that Marla and I never had any disagreements between us, it was between Jared and her. I wrote her a letter and asked if we could just forget about the past and be friends again, be the family we actually were, but I didn't know her address so I gave the letter to Eileen so she could pass it on to Marla. I got a note back, or a card saying "mind your own business", and that was final, the end of our friendship. That was when I lost my "sister" and my niece the year of 1996.

My father and I got closer than ever and I was so happy that dad finally accepted Jared. It had been a heavy burden for me to be in the middle of the two men in my life, the men I loved. One didn't want me to be with the other, and the other tried to make me choose, but I didn't want to choose between my father and fiancé. I believed in peace and I wanted to have them both.

We started to become the closest what I would call a family we had ever been, so when Liza, my father's girlfriend told me she was expecting and that I was going to have a sibling, I was happy for them. Liza refused to have a baby outside of marriage and so my father decided to marry her. The wedding was set to New Year's Eve 1990 in London and this time, both Jared and I were invited and my father set everything up for us to travel to London, and the hotel, everything. We were so excited and I was very, very happy.

My sister was not going to make this trip and it felt good that I was the one going. There would be, of course, because it was my father, upscale dresses and suits, but to find a dress in my size would not be easy. I went to the one and only nice boutique I knew in Gothenburg and found two dresses and one pair of shoes. I couldn't make up my mind which one to take and I didn't think we could afford both, but when Jared came with me a few days later, he told me to take both dresses and the shoes.

We traveled to London and one night when we were at my father's apartment, Liza told us they'd found out the sex of the baby; it was a boy. I smiled because finally my father would have the boy he always wanted whom he could name John. Dad had wanted both Annie and I to be "John" when our mother expected us, but we were girls.

New Year's Eve and the wedding day came and because the bride was dressed in off-white, it was okay for me to wear my white dress and blue shoes. I normally don't wear tight clothes because of my figure, but this dress was form-fitting and I looked stunning. When we arrived at the venue, I could see in my father's eyes that he appreciated how I looked and he was proud of me. Dad embraced both Jared and me and thanked us so much for coming. Liza and my dad had their reception at the restaurant on the roof at the luxurious London Hilton and it was wonderful!

Their wedding song was the theme song from *The Godfather*, which didn't surprise anyone; it was my father's favorite movie. At the table, I had Jared on one side and dad's business partner Anders who was from Norway, on the other. Anders was younger than dad, and a few years older than I. He was tall, handsome and a real gentleman; something I was not use to and it felt nice. Jared and I spoke to him a lot, we took pictures and I also danced with him. The whole night turned out to be very nice and magical for me. I felt like a princess and was delighted when it was time to say thank you and goodbye for the night. I got a genuine hug and a kiss on my cheek from Anders before it was my father's turn to embrace me.

"Thank you honey," dad said, "you look absolutely fabulous tonight. It means a lot to me to have you here today."

Completely thrilled with the evening I started to get ready for bed when Jared said,

"So have you and Anders had anything together?"

Just like Cinderella at midnight, Jared now busted my happy bubble.

"What?"

"You heard me."

"No we haven't, it's the first time I have met him."

"It looks like Anders likes you."

"Anders was nice, but he is my father's partner and I'm engaged to you Jared."

"Because he is your dad's partner doesn't mean a shit, does it? You know how his friends can be."

Right away I knew Jared was referring to Jim who raped me when I was 13 years old. It wasn't fair at all to bring that up like it was my fault, but I didn't say anything more, it would only make the situation worse. Most of the trip turned out well, we were hanging out mostly with my uncle and Liza's mother Dana, who was staying at the same hotel as we were. Dad and Jared had words once on this trip, but they soon worked it out because of all the other people around.

When my father first moved to Spain, it took years before Jared and I got the opportunity to visit with him and his family there. August 1993 was the first time we went to visit my father in Spain and at this point, my father and Liza had gotten another son so now I had two younger brothers on my father's side. First, it was John and now Carl was born a year and a half after. The first time Jared and I saw Carl, he was only 8 months old. We had such a great time and started to go there every year for vacation.

On our third trip, at a party at my father's house, Jared and my father got into a big argument when Jared acted like a jerk. He disrespected my father in his home and in front of his friends. It ended with Jared and I staying away from their house for the last days of that trip.

The following year, I hadn't spoken with my father and Jared had told me that I would have to choose; it was either my dad or him. Jared already knew I would stay with him. Knowing my father, he is a very strong minded man as well, and would never come to Jared and apologize so things were at a dead end. I was incredibly sad about it, but did my best to brush it off and focus on my life with Jared. We went to Spain anyway that summer although I didn't want to, but Jared insisted saying,

"It's not the Porno King's country, you know."

It wasn't that I thought my father owned Spain, but to be so close and still so far from him, it would break my heart. Jared didn't care so we went there as real tourists; stayed in a hotel and had a rental car. My father didn't even know we were there until he and Liza drove by us on the street, but still we didn't speak with each other. I missed him and my brothers very much, but I didn't say a word to Jared, it would just make him annoyed.

The following year, I hadn't spoken to my father for two years. It was time for another vacation to Marbella, Spain. Jared told me we were going to go to my dad's house so Jared could apologize to him. I was surprised and happy but I was also nervous of how dad would react. We went to his house for his birthday and the gate to their yard was already open so we drove in, parked the car and rang the doorbell. Liza opened the door and when she saw it was us she asked with an attitude,

"What do you want and why are you here?"

"We are here to say happy birthday to my dad. Is he here and can we come in?"

"Yes, your father is here."

She stepped aside so we could go in. My father was downstairs, sitting on the couch with his back to us and didn't see us walking down the stairs.

"Eric, someone is here to talk to you," Liza said.

Dad turned around and looked at us without saying a word. It was very nice to see my father again, but he looked so much older than when I saw him the last time. He was already drunk although it was only early afternoon.

"Hey daddy and happy birthday," I said while I handed over the present from my sister and me.

Now Jared opened his mouth.

> "Eric, we came here to say happy birthday and also to say I'm sorry for being so aggressive last time we talked. Just because we disagree with each other doesn't mean we have to be enemies, but the alcohol got into both of us I guess. Hannah and I, especially Hannah, have been very sad for what happened and I would like for us to be friends again."

My dad looked first at me and back at Jared,

> "Apology accepted and thank you for my gift."

The gift was a picture taken at a studio of a professional photograph of my sister and me; my sister dressed in white, me in black. After that, we hung out with them almost the whole trip and we also got invited to dad's 48th birthday party. There were a lot of people whom I have never met, and some that I've seen before. I had a conversation to one of their friend, Kim whom I met before, and she told us she started to design jewelry and invited us to stop by to see what she had before going back to Sweden.

When we did, Kim showed us some beautiful rings, but all of them were too big for my small fingers. I eventually saw a ring that I really liked; it wasn't as big as the others, gold with a big ruby in the middle with six smaller rubies and nine smaller diamonds. I tried it on and from that moment, I didn't want to take it off. It looked like it was made for me and I looked at Jared and he looked at my hand.

> "You like it huh?"

> "No Jared, I love it."

We asked how much Kim was asking for it and once again we looked at each other.

"Can we please buy it Jared? It can be my new engagement ring because you've already lost yours. Please? When we get married, both of us will get rings again."

I had a huge smile on my face and when Jared said okay, I gave him a warm hug.

"Thank you, I love it!"

Meeting with old friends

I hadn't seen Monica in years when I ran into her sister-in-law at the gas station where I was working at the time. I asked how Monica was doing and got her telephone number again, so I called as soon as I got home and Monica was happy to hear from me again. We chatted about this and that, caught up on recent events and Monica told me she lived with her boyfriend now, who was one of Jared childhood friends.

"What? Are you kidding me Mon?"

"No Hannah, Jared and Benny were neighbors and used to hang out all the time, just as we did. All the other neighbors in that whole block, used to call Jared the 'Ruby Street terror', because when something bad happened, Jared was involved," Monica said and continued, "Do you remember when we always hung out Hannah?"

"Of course I remember; best times of my life. Let's keep in touch now Mon, I've missed you so much."

"Yes, for sure baby girl!"

When Jared came home, I asked him about this 'Benny' and he told me that they had been good friends and when Benny's family moved, the two boys lost contact. This made me hopeful that maybe the friendship would be renewed when Jared got in touch with his friend again, and with Benny's girl friend being my best friend, all four of us would be able to hang out together.

Benny and Jared talked a few times on the phone and we made plans to go up to visit them one weekend. They had bought a house together in a great location and I loved it from the beginning. It was decorated cozy with warm colors and we had a great reunion that evening. I could see Monica was happy and since the last time I saw her, she had lost a whole lot of weight. She looked great!

When I next spoke with Monica, I asked her if she and Benny wanted to go out to dinner and then to a club. After she talked with Benny, Monica said they'd love to. We met halfway, and went to dinner and had a few drinks. We all got a little tipsy but since none of us drove, we would be fine and could relax. We were just about to catch a cab, when Jared and Benny started to argue about nothing, and neither of them wanted to admit that he was wrong or back down. So the argument went on until some old stuff came up, which surprised me. Benny told Jared,

> "You're just like you were when you were a kid. I thought you might have grown up, but no Jared, you are exactly the same."

Benny took Monica's hand and said,

> "Come honey, let's catch a cab home."

I was just standing there too surprised to say anything when Jared said with his usual attitude,

> "Are you just going to stand there all night? I'm leaving."

> "But what happened, why . . ."

Jared cut me off,

> "Because Benny is a fucking nothing. He has always been a little chicken; scared as hell of me!"

"Are we going home Jared?"

"The night is young, let's go to the Avenue."

We went into a club and I could see that he already had too many drinks but Jared ordered one more anyway. I decided I would not have another and declined, and then Jared just left me standing there all by myself, knowing I wasn't comfortable at all. All these years we had been together, Jared had trodden on my self-esteem and times like this made me feel even worse. He danced with everyone but me and when Jared had enjoyed himself enough he decided it was time to go home. We took a taxi and I prayed that he would fall asleep when we got home and fortunate my prayers were answered!

I was concerned about the situation with Monica and Benny. Maybe I was wishing this reunion between Jared, Benny, Monica and me would work and had gotten my hopes up too much. *'I have to call her tomorrow,'* that was the last thing on my mind before I fell asleep.

The following day, I woke up early and when it was 10:00 am, I couldn't wait any longer, and called Monica. She was short in her answers and I heard it in her voice, things had changed between us again. Monica confirmed that Benny didn't want to deal with Jared anymore because of his unstable personality. I was so sad and had a real heartache when we hang up. Once again I had lost a very close friend because of Jared.

As time passed, we just got lonelier and lonelier when our friends one after the other distanced themselves from us because of Jared's aggressiveness and erratic behavior. Because of that, Jared and I were spending most of our time by ourselves. This meant that he found more opportunities to harass me in all kinds of different ways and more opportunities to beat me up. It was one thing after the other; staying up at night to keep him company, even though I had to go to work the following morning. Or I had to use all my strength to stay quiet while he raped me, pinched me, kicked me or played "head banger" on my forehead. This, often because something he tried to do, didn't work his way.

If Jared couldn't find a paper he had put away; it was my fault. If the laundry room was busy because our neighbors were using it; it was my fault. If his allergy was bothering him; it was of course because of me. Jared could always find a reason, and the fault was always mine. He was simply a raving lunatic!

A few months following the situation with Benny, Jared got fired from one of his jobs, when he was fortunate to get an opportunity to take his license to drive a bus. It was a 12-week course. He would get paid fulltime and get his bus driver's license, so it was a great deal.

Jared became friendly with a girl in his class and they would constantly interact during school hours. After only a week, Jared and this girl Beth, would get together after school also and during this entire time he usually ignored me. He was often an hour or more late, and sometimes even happened to 'forget' to pick me up from work. I had to take the bus home because Jared didn't or wouldn't answer his cell or call me back when I left messages. Beth took priority over me and when I brought it up, he told me 'they're just studying', or he was helping her out by giving her a ride home, even though Beth lived the opposite direction from where we lived. I was hurt, and of course jealous when my fiancé total ignored me! Jared would say it was my own fault that he was spending time with other people and not me. He would ask,

"Who wants to be around someone who's just nagging all day long, and doesn't trust me? Who wants somebody as fat as you when I can have someone slim and sexy."

There was absolutely nothing sexy about me and Jared enjoyed taunting me with, 'even your own father is ashamed of his daughters, and how fat and ugly my sister and I were. Although my father looked like a pig himself,' as Jared said. And yes, my father did tell me once when I was 18 . . .

"Hannah, let's talk for a minute. You are so overweight and if you don't lose weight, Jared is going to kick you to the curb for someone who is skinny and pretty."

"I don't believe so because Jared loves me," I answered.

In the back of my head I knew Jared's 'love' was obsessive and controlling. All he wanted was to own and control me. Instead of kicking me to the curb, Jared knew he could do whatever he wanted to me, and still know I wouldn't leave him. I was too scared of him, so Jared could 'have his cake and eat it too', so to speak.

When Jared nagged about it, I start to gain even more weight. I didn't want to be this big; it wasn't healthy and I knew it, but it was a way for me to protect myself. Honestly, I didn't eat much, but I was 'comfort eating' and ate the wrong things, nothing healthy. All the bottled up stress made it impossible for me to focus and lose weight. Jared who always complained about my weight when he was in a bad mood, was encouraging me to eat the wrong things when everything was good. He would say diets are not good and one has to work out to get the weight off, but Jared never gave me the time to do it. He kept me busy with things he thought were important to him, without ever taking into consideration what was best for me.

Finally Jared's bus driving instruction was completed and he got his driver's license. All his classmates went their separate ways, but he still had contact with Beth. Then after a while, she was not interested in him any longer, I guess. It was time for him to look for a job at Line Express Bus; one of the two companies that ran the city buses in Gothenburg and they were hiring graduates from that school. Jared's chance of getting a job was good, and there was a plus as the bus company was next door to the gas station where I worked. The drivers and the people in the office knew me very well and liked me a lot, and I arranged a job interview between the office manager and Jared.

Jared liked the job and it paid reasonably well although he was hired on an hourly basis, but hourly work was always available and eventually the job became a fulltime job. I was happy and thought that maybe now we would get our finances in order because we both were working.

It was July 28, 1996 and Jared and I, had just been arguing about one thing or the other, when I went out on the balcony for a smoke. While out there, I was thinking about our relationship and if there was anything I could do to make things better? To be closer to a loving relationship in action and not in words with no follow through; to see some improvement, at least. Jared hated when I smoked, so I came up with an idea. I had only five cigarettes left in the pack so after I finished the cigarette, I went back into the apartment to share my thoughts with Jared, who was in the shower.

"Hey Jared, I have a proposal for you. You want to make a bet?"

"A bet about what?"

"I know how much you hate when I smoke and right now, I only have five cigarettes left. I will smoke them, but after that I will make an effort to stop, and you will stop beating me up."

"Sounds fair. Yeah, we can do that."

I did finish my cigarettes and have never touched one since, but Jared continued the same way as before; he never stopped the abuse.

OPENED HIS OWN KARATE STUDIO

Jared had been practicing karate for years and had now advanced to a Black Belt. That meant Jared was allowed to open his own karate-studio and teach self-defense. This was in 1997 and we had talked about it for a while, on and off, back and forth. We had saved up some money and finally it was time for him to make one of his dreams come true; to start his own studio. The location was an easy choice, Öckerö one of the islands, and a community to Gothenburg, where his older sister and her family lived. We would call it ISD, Islands Self Defense. His nephews wanted to take lessons and there were no self-defense schools located in the area. The residents who had an interest in karate lessons had to go all the way downtown

Gothenburg, so the area seemed well suited, and we both believed it would be successful.

We surveyed the neighborhood and some residents were thrilled, while other residents were against it, but we were determined. As with all new start-up companies, there was a lot of advertising, flyers, and other paperwork that needed to be done and filed before Jared could get the karate studio off the ground. I helped him and supported him in all issues. There were some people out on the islands that didn't want anything "violent" like karate in the area, in what they called their "safe zone". But by following and meeting all the zoning laws and codes, and having various talks and meetings with the Budo Alliance, it was finally time for opening day. The class schedule would be three different classes every day; one for kids, one for women only, and one for both men and women. The classes would run back to back.

We were in business and lessons started. I would hear Jared instruct his students, telling them the rules about karate and that it's only to be used in self-defense. Meaning of course; *not* to be used for showing off to your friends, *not* to be used as a bullying tool to threaten *or* to beat someone up.

I already knew that, of course, but for me to hear Jared educate this and being abused by him at home, it was unbelievable! Even though I never practiced karate, I didn't like it but it was most likely because of my terrifying experience with Jared.

A year after Jared got his license to drive a bus, I took the same tests and I got my license to drive a bus.

The school only accepted thirteen people and I was the only woman in the class, but I felt quite comfortable. Most of the men had been driving trucks before so driving big vehicles like this was somewhat familiar to them. I had never driven anything bigger than a moving truck, so the first time I was allowed to drive a bus, I was awfully nervous and unsure of myself as I am only five feet tall but surprisingly it went very well. I liked the classes, but enjoyed practicing the driving most of all.

For the first time in my life, I was in control of something and I did great! The theory was somewhat difficult and I had to gain knowledge of how to change bus tires and how to put snow chains on the bus. I also had to learn the workings of the engine, the fuel system etc. I had never done this on my own vehicle, but in order to get a passing grade, I had to know how to do it. By staying focused and listening in class and a lot of hard work, finally it was time for the final test. I got stuck on some questions but continued on, then went back to try to answer the questions I skipped and at the end, I did answer all of the questions. The following day we got the results and we were told only one person didn't make it. I was sure that person was I and began feeling sad. The teacher continued,

"A few more of you wouldn't have made it if we didn't eliminate one question. Eleven of you had the wrong answer. We therefore had to look back on the question and ask if we formulated the question incorrectly."

Both teachers then decided to take that question off the test and when I got my test back, on the top it read 'passed'. That disqualified question was a break for me and that is why I passed. That day, fate smiled on me.

The manager at Line Express Bus had already told me I had a job if I passed. My last day at school was Friday, and Monday I started my new job as a city bus driver.

The company had another driver train me for about two weeks, showing me the routes, and then it was time to do it on my own. I loved my job and I got plenty of hours, even though the shifts were split. Some days my first shift would be between 4:30 a.m. to 9:30 a.m. and then the second shift would start at 2:30 p.m. or 6:00 p.m. or 10:00 p.m. I still loved my job.

All my life I've been working with people and that's what I do best; I make people feel welcomed and safe. After a while the passengers started to recognize me and they were happy to see me. Not only because I was on time, but they were happy to see a female bus driver. I got compliments from everyone, from co-workers and from passengers, men, women and kids. I felt so appreciated.

Everyone at work knew that Jared and I were together as a couple. Jared behaved well and was very sweet and they loved him at first. At home, Jared was still as controlling and obsessed about things as always. Both of us had a very easy time talking with people and made some new friends at work. Lottie and Gerald, two of them, became our best friends. They had met at work and started dating. After a while the four of us hung out whenever Jared took the time and I started to be happy again. Finally we had some new friends. I thought that would make things easier than with my old friends. Gerald and Lottie accepted Jared for who he was, or for whom they thought he was, and not because he was my fiancé.

A few months later Lottie told me, she had something to tell me and didn't want me to be sad. Lottie said she and Gerald were going to have a baby; she was pregnant and in her third month. I again felt the emptiness in my heart like the times before when I thought and wanted so badly to have a baby, but I was happy for them. Lottie was my best friend and we talked about everything. Well, almost everything, because I never told her what a hell I was living at home and how Jared abused me.

Lottie had told me about her ex-boyfriend who abused her once and how she felt about men like that. I knew if Lottie found out, she and Gerald would withdraw and wouldn't want to be around us anymore. I didn't want to risk losing another set of friends, so I didn't say a word.

Lottie delivered a baby girl, Jen, and everything went great. Even though Lottie and Gerald were now new parents, they always welcomed us to their home and I spent a lot of time there when Jared went to ISD. Their daughter got to know me and every time I went there, Jen would be glued to me and the little girl became very attached to me. When Jen start talking, she didn't call me Hannah, it was "my Hannah". I was so flattered.

Lottie's family had a little get-together with a few people at their home. There was drinking although Lottie didn't drink because she was expecting another baby only a few months after Jen was born and I was the designated driver, but we all had a good time. One of the guests was Rick, he was a co-worker and has been a good friend of Gerald for some time. Jared had a few drinks, more like one too many, and I saw the other side of him starting to bleed through with his attitude towards Rick. Jared had told me before that he thought Rick was retarded and stupid, but of course, Jared had never told Gerald that. So now, Jared told Rick what he thought about him and he was teasing him in front of everyone until Gerald stepped in and pulled Jared aside and asked him to stop. Jared continued towards Rick, so Gerald asked him to leave. Lottie came over to me and said,

"You are more than welcome to stay, but as long as Jared doesn't know how to behave, he is not welcome here."

"I understand, but I can't stay if Jared leaves."

From the look Lottie gave me, I know she saw the fright in my eyes. Again I felt the anxiety begin in my stomach as we left their house, I would never dare to stay without him.

When next I spoke to Lottie, she asked me if Jared always behaved like that when he drank.

"Not always," I answered, "but quite often and most of the time towards me, but not as often with others."

Jared apologized to Rick and Gerald when he saw them again and said he had too many drinks, and his apology was accepted. After that incident, when Lottie and I were by ourselves, she started to ask me if everything was okay at home.

"Yeah, it's just fine," I lied and felt like an idiot, but I didn't want her to turn away from me because of him.

"Is Jared ever aggressive towards you Hannah?"

"Sometimes he is," I changed the subject quickly and said, "Look at Jen, how cute is she?"

I didn't want her to ask more questions about how Jared was towards me.

Lottie was a stay-home mom but Gerald, Jared and I were still working at Line Express Bus.

I was now on the job for eighteen months and every day I would get a headache that lasted all day. I went to see a doctor to find out what was wrong and I was scared as one of my mother's friends had died from a brain tumor a short time before.

When my mother last visited with her friend, she told my mother about how she had been having a terrible headache for weeks. When the friend went to the doctor, she was told that she had cancer and six months later mom's friend passed away. That is why I waited as long as I could stand it before I finally went to see Dr. Jonson.

I was scared for what the answer might be. He told me it was stress and I needed some physical therapy to learn how to stretch my neck muscles, especially because I was using certain muscles while driving the bus. Dr. Jonson put me on the sick list for a month so my condition would get a chance to improve.

Now that I was at home all day, Jared put me to work there. I was working on paperwork for ISD, putting information lists together and planned future events. Among my tasks was to make sure there was no laundry to be done, and that our apartment was clinically clean at all times. Over the years, I had acquired the habit of failing to put his things away, so I put all his papers in a pile on the kitchen desk. When Jared looked through the paperwork and couldn't find what he was looking for, he would wake me if I were sleeping to find whatever he was looking for. If I couldn't find it, he would put me through hell.

Meanwhile, Jared was flirting with one of the girls at work, and he had the nerve to ask her out to dinner even though everyone there knew we were engaged.

It was already rumored that Jared was cheating on me and some of the guys went as far as to stop talking to him. Everyone in the office as well as the bus drivers loved me and called me "Line Express Bus Little Sunshine". Everyone's attitude and reaction towards Jared started to affect him and almost every day there was some disagreement at work. No one at the company liked how Jared was treating me and they did not hesitate to give him a piece of their mind and, of course, it turned out to be my fault that he was treated badly.

At first, I didn't understand why our coworkers shunned him, but a few months later I got the answer when Lottie told me about Danica. Gerald and Lottie had known about it since it happened, but they hadn't said anything to me, trying to shield me from the hurt.

I got very upset, not only at Jared, but also at Lottie and Gerald because they didn't told me right away. Don't let me be the last to know! I had heard rumors and gossip that Jared was flirting with Danica and was interested in her, but she liked another guy and knew Jared was my fiancé. Whatever really happened, I will never find out as the only ones who knows the truth are Jared and Danica. Shortly after this happened, we both stopped working at the bus company. Jared, because according to him, everyone was either stupid, jerks, or had an attitude, and I quit because Jared said so.

"No reason for you to stay around those jerks who are just trying to put bullshit about me in my head."

PARTYING WITH OUR COWORKERS

A few months after we stopped working for the bus company Jared was hired by a taxi company. When his two bosses met me, they asked him if I wanted to work for the company as well and I gladly accepted. Our schedules were days, but we didn't get enough hours, so we switched and took the graveyard shift instead; worked from 6:00

p.m. until 6:00 a.m., seven days a week. It was fun and there were not many bad incidents with people even for me, a woman driving a taxi. When there was a problem, a coworker was always somewhere close by that could come quickly to my aid. Jared and I knew the city well and got many customers who asked for us when they needed a cab. This caused jealousy among coworkers, but we ignored it.

Jared and Michael, a coworker, didn't know each other well, or if at all, but for some reason they couldn't stand each other. I think it was because Michael was laid back and didn't care about anything but himself and spoke his mind.

In the first years after I started dating Jared, I used to go out with my girl friends from time to time, and Jared encouraged me to do so. Most of the time, he came and picked me up when it was time to go home. Those times, we even drove my girlfriends home and they would tell me 'I was so lucky to have such a nice boyfriend.' I would smile and respond with 'Yeah, I know,' and only I knew!

Shortly thereafter I found out it was better for me not to go out even though I had a great time with my friends. Every time I would go out, not only partying but anywhere, Jared would ask me how it was? Not only did he ask; I had to describe in detail what we did from the time he dropped me off until he picked me up. If I didn't remember, well I had better, otherwise Jared would torture and keep me up until I did summon up the event. "No one could have such a bad memory not to remember," he said. According to Jared, it wasn't just my body that was so fat, my brain was too, and he was more than happy to remind me of it every opportunity he got, or he made one up.

From time to time Jared would ask me the same questions day after day. He would even wait a few weeks and ask me again, and if there was anything I was hesitating about or anything said differently from the first time, another fight was on.

"Jared can't you see how crazy this is?" I would tell him. "Do you really believe I would have the nerve to lie to you? You beat me up when I am telling you the truth so what would you do if I lied to you? Kill me?"

"What are you talking about? I don't hit you; just teach you a little lesson so you'll learn how to behave. You have a wild imagination. I haven't touched you, Hannah."

With all that, I stopped going out with my friends, except when it was a extra special occasion, and Jared told me people would be wondering why I didn't show up to one event or another. Even Jared realized they would probably speculate that it was because he wasn't going to come with us so he figured it looked better if I attended some event. When I did go out it was just for me to enjoy that very moment while hanging out with the girls and do my best to forget about what I had ahead of me when I got home. I think that's what the spiritual people call, "living in the now."

Some of our coworkers at the taxi company planned on going out, have a few drinks and just relax. We were all working seven days/nights a week and 10-12 hour shifts so we needed some down time. They invited us to go with them but we said no thanks; we needed the money and even though it was a weekday, it could get very busy for us and that meant we would make good money.

"Hannah, you should go with them," Jared told me.

I was tempting to go but told him,

"No. I don't really feel like going. Why do you want me to go?"

"It will be quiet tonight so go and chill with them while I am working. Call me when you want to go home and I'll pick you up."

They had decide they were going to meet at Michael's house, have a drink and from there go to the bar downtown Gothenburg. I thought to myself, 'Just great!' Because of how Jared felt about Michael, it wasn't a good idea for me to go to his house and I told Jared I would meet them at the bar instead.

"Oh no Hannah. You are going to Michael's house like everyone else or you don't go at all. I trust you."

"What?"

"You don't trust yourself?" Jared continued.

"Jared you are tripping! I love you and would never do anything to hurt you or make you upset."

He dropped me at Michael's house and no one else but Michael himself was there when I arrived. He poured us both a drink while I took a tour of his apartment; it was actually very comfortable. This was the first time I got a chance to really talk to Michael and get a chance to know him better. Before it had always been at the taxi stations while we were waiting for customers and there was only time for chitchat, not time to get to know a person.

Michael was actually sweet, which surprised me. Nadina, the other girl who was coming with us, called him and said she was running late so if we didn't mind, it was better if we met down at the bar. Michael looked at me and I said that was fine, "I can call Jared and he'll give us a ride to the bar." Jared was still close by and was more than happy to drive us there. I was worried about how the guys would get along in the car, but I was worried for no reason it seemed. Jared and Michael actually had a good conversation, it made me calmer and more comfortable and I thought that maybe the arguments between them would now stop. Forty-five minutes later Jared dropped us off at *The Stairs*, he gave me a kiss and wished us a nice evening. We didn't have to pay cover charge as our company referred many customers to the club. While at the coat checkroom, the attendant asked if she could put our jackets on the same hanger and we both said that was okay. I looked around for Nadina and Alex and they were already there waiting by a table and waiving at us.

"Hey Michael and Hannah, we are over here."

We gave them a hug and greeted them while we sat down and ordered a drink. This was the first, and it turned out to be the last time, I saw any of our coworkers socially outside of work. We had a great time, talking, drinking and dancing but around 1:00 a.m. it was time for us start thinking about headed home. We asked for the check and went to get our jackets. When the girl handed us the jackets, Michael took them both, put his on first and helped me to put on my jacket, as a gentleman should. I gave him a hug and said thank you. I looked over his shoulder and exactly at that time, the door opened and Jared walked in.

Our eyes met and as I looked into his eyes, Jared had that crazy look I knew all too well. His eyes were pitch black and my heart suddenly started to race and my body shaking as if I was having a panic attack. I could see people talking around me, but I couldn't hear what they were saying. It sounded like they were far away. I got the feeling, the thought, whatever, that Jared was going to kill Michael or me.

"What the fuck . . ." While he grabbed my jacket and threw me towards the exit.

I was scared Jared was going to destroy Michael, but he just looked at him, snaring between his teeth

"You're dead, dickhead!" and then came right at me.

Daniel, another coworker was there and we started to walk down the stairs when Jared kicked me at the back of my knee. I tried not to fall so I grabbed Daniel's arm, the coworker who brought Jared over there. Daniel looked at Jared . . .

"Take it easy man."

"Shut your fucking mouth and let go of my little slut's arm. She's only getting what she deserves," he said with obnoxious attitude.

Daniel and I were good friends and so far, Jared liked him too. Daniel and his friends always used to call me when they were going out partying but he had no clue how Jared treated and controlled me. Jared's car wasn't running and that was why the two of them came to get the keys to my taxicab so Jared could work the last few hours. Daniel dropped us where my taxicab was parked, and when I got out of the car, he looked at me and I saw the concern in his face.

"Are you going to be all right?"

My eyes were mirrored, reflecting the fear I felt, and Daniel saw it but didn't do anything. Daniel left and Jared said,

"Get your fat ass up there before I put myself in trouble," as soon as he parked the car outside the building where we lived.

"So you're not going out anymore tonight?" I asked with low voice.

"It's not your business bitch. Do you ask so the little Michael can come rescue you?"

"Come on Jared, you know it's not like that."

"What do I know? You say you're going out partying with friends and next thing you do is fucking a coworker."

"Jared, we didn't do anything! I gave Michael a hug when he put the jacket on me and that's all! What happen after that you already know you were there; that was when you walked in."

"But what if I hadn't showed up? Then you would have gone home and fucked him while I was out working my ass off for us."

While I walked up the stairs, I prayed that Jared was going out a few more hours before he started to torture me for something I hadn't done. I already knew he would, but I had no clue how bad and for how long I would have to be punished and suffer for something that never happened.

My body was shaking in anticipation and not knowing what was going to happen when we got home. I mean, I know Jared was going to beat me up, or teach me a lesson. Teach me how to behave right or whatever else he felt like calling it, but I can't describe the feeling in my body while I got closer and closer our apartment. Can you imagine how it would feel to walk to your own execution? That is how I felt! I was thinking, *'This is how it must feel for someone who is facing a death penalty, an innocent man, wrongfully charged,'* but honestly in this instance, with these facts . . . . dying would have been less painful for me than to go through what I had to go through for the years to come.

As soon as we got into our apartment, the first thing Jared did was to tell me to get undressed so he can take a look at me while he figure out 'how a fat hooker like you should be punished.' Those were his exact words.

"Please Jared, don't do this. Let me go to bed and you can go out finish your shift and let us talk about this tomorrow okay?"

What I tried to do was to buy some time, and to give Jared some time so he could calm down at least a little bit.

"What the fuck, you little taxi fucker." This also became his nickname for me. "You trying to get rid of me so you can call Michael to come save you? He don't want you Hannah, he just wanted some pussy. No one wants you!" he shook his head. "What make you think anyone would want a fatso like you? Michael, Alex and Nadina is probably laughing at your fat ass right now but you are too stupid to understand that, huh?"

Jared had that arrogant smile on his face that I've had come to hate so much. It's the smile of control and power, saying 'You are mine and I can do whatever I want to you. There is no one who can help or save you! You're mine forever!' Whenever Jared had that smile, I always knew something bad was going to happen.

I got undressed but left my panties and bra on and when he saw that he said,

"Oh it is disgusting to see you naked, you look like a pig, and it makes me want to throw up. Take the rest off too and go to bed."

For a moment I thought Jared was actually going to give me time to rest and time for him to calm down, that was until I saw him start to take his pants off and the last thing I was in mood for right then was sex.

"Suck my dick bitch and do it as good as you did Michael."

"But Jared . . ." was all he gave me a chance to say before he pulled my hair and twisted it around so hard it flipped me over on my back while he whispered, "There is no but Jared, and please doesn't help no more. Now get your fat ass up here and show me how you did Michael."

Instead of doing what Jared told me to do, I crawled under the cover to hide my body and tried to hide myself when his fist landed on my ear. My ear started beeping and I got the taste of blood in my mouth. DAMN that hurts and I had to bite my lip so I wouldn't scream; that would make him even angrier.

"You must really enjoy this, taxi fucker, but I have no time to play games with you." He continued, "I need to go out and make some money while my wife is out fucking and she's not even getting paid. You're not even smart enough to make money while you're out fucking around, but I guess no one would pay you anyway huh? What's the saying, pussy is a pussy, and the dick has no eyes! Now get your fat ass up here."

He grabbed the skin on the side of my hips and pulled me up in 'doggy style,' forced his penis in between my legs and start pounding hard and fast. Was Jared thinking if it was hurting me? Of course he did! Jared didn't even care if it felt good for him or that I was dry as a desert as long as it did hurt and humiliated me. That was the whole purpose for him, to hurt me.

My tears was slowly falling, running down my cheeks, the whole time and I prayed to God that Jared would be done quick and it would be over soon. After that, he would leave me alone for at least a few hours while he was working, and if not, he could continue for hours with harassing and abusing me. He came, pulled out and said,

"You are such a whore."

He kicked my side and I fell down on the bed again. I looked at him as he walked out of the room.

Without a word, he was getting ready to leave, and I got under the covers again. I felt some relief in my body, my stomach, my heart and my soul when I heard him close and lock the door. Once again I thanked God for sparing my life, for giving me a little break before his next attack. I prayed for someone to come and help me. I always prayed for that, but it just felt like there was no one in the entire world that could help me out of this situation. Jared had total control and I was sure he was the devil.

After that, I was scared of just being on the same taxicab station as Michael because Jared could show up at any time. Even though I was in my car and Michael was in his, we were still "fucking" each other every time, according to Jared. Those two couldn't stand each other and one thing that pissed Jared off even more was that Michael didn't back down from him, he talked back and Jared wasn't used to that.

GOT OUR COMPUTER

At last we had the money, or we made it a priority to buy our own computer. I guess it was a relief for both of his sisters because now we didn't have to bother either of them to use or have them do something for us. Additionally, it would help me as I was planning to start my own business. We were extremely excited to get started with our computer and as soon as we installed it, I started to play with it. It was about two months since I finished computer classes; Thank God for that. Before that, I didn't have a clue about anything having to do with computers.

Now, Jared had me working almost all my free time on the computer. It was everything from weekly information about training, individual letters to monthly magazine for ISD. He was working and training almost seven days a week with doing his individual training as well as train his students, and I was left to take care of our house, bills and most of the paper work for the studio. All this and hold down my own job, so we were constantly busy all the time. Using the internet we could start to make international contacts and market his karate business. Jared begun to use the chat rooms online and told me how much fun it was and showed me how to do it.

JARED USED MY HEAD FROM TIME TO TIME AS . . .

Jared was good in karate; he had great technique and could easily break 15 bricks with his forehead. From time to time, when Jared thought I deserved it, he practiced with my forehead instead of the bricks. On this occasion, Jared blamed me because our car wouldn't start and he couldn't be at the studio on time. I knew something bad was going to happen. Jared started to argue with me, saying I was too lazy, too fat and simply too everything negative because I couldn't figure out what was wrong with the car. When he finally gave up and we went back up to our apartment, he was in a terrible mood.

> "Bitch what do you think I should do now? Just cancel the practice and let my students down? No! You got to come up with something and quick!"

I felt stress and panic coming over me; I felt the anxiety rising in my stomach and my breathing was short. I closed my eyes, took a deep breath and told myself to remain calm and think. Think! To not panic, think and stay focused.

There were times when I thought that Jared had changed and I believed he would be and act responsibly. Now he had his own studio and students, and I wished that he would take his own advice and obey the rules he was teaching his students. Then at other times, like this time, I realized Jared hadn't changed. *Not one bit!*

"I don't know what to do Jared, but it's not my fault the car won't start."

Jared turned around quickly, crossed his arms over his chest and walked directly towards me.

"I don't give a shit if you have to go steal a car, but you're coming up with a solution NOW."

Bang! I wasn't expecting that.

My forehead started to swell immediately and I had the taste of blood in my mouth. I just looked helplessly at him through my tears. I couldn't even say anything because it would only make the situation worse. The pain in my head was indescribable but I felt even more pain in my heart and soul. How can Jared do something like this to someone he claims he loves? And how can I be with someone who has been treating me like this for twelve years? I was still hoping for a miracle. Hoping that someone would come and rescue me from this hell. Or hoping that Jared would grow up, stop beating me and act like a normal human being.

Twelve years is a very long time. An especially long time, enough time to create fear and insecurity in someone and to be quite sure that person won't find a way out and leave you.

Jared called his students and did cancel the karate class that night, he couldn't find a way to get there on time. The students understood; it can happen to anyone, they said. I wished we could have figured out a way to get to the karate studio, and I knew it would be a long, painful evening with him at home. I closed my eyes for a minute and prayed to God that I would survive this night.

We didn't have any friends who we could call to give him a ride; this was because Jared had a hard time sometimes controlling his temper. When that happened, our friends backed off and stayed away from us. Jared always expected our friends to be there for us especially when we needed a favor, but it was under his conditions and according to his rules and wishes, and when he wanted something done.

We struggled to get the karate studio up and running and to get people to know we were there and after only a month, we had a few members who became regulars and took the classes week after week. This was due to good word-of-mouth marketing and having an organization in a small town like Öckerö. If people like something, they'll talk about it and others will come to investigate what it is all about. Jared had such great ideas, I thought from the beginning, and wanted to involve the members more and more in the studio. Therefore, we figured out all kinds of different activities in which to involve the members.

For example; the students who were helping us sell Bingo tickets would make some money that they could use towards karate expenses, such as the camps, guards etc, and the more tickets you sold the more money you made. Two girls were truly lucky, their parents owned the biggest candy store on the island and sold the tickets in the store for their girls. The tickets were sold up to a specific cut off time within we could call in the numbers, and the unsold tickets could be returned.

Early in this enterprise, all the tickets were sold out and we didn't have to pay for the unsold tickets, but after a few weeks Jared got greedy.

"Let's just keep all the unsold tickets and let ISD pay for them. Who knows, there might be a winning ticket that we are returning. How would you feel then knowing we returned the winning ticket for a car or the biggest price ever."

"Well I don't know because what if there are no winning tickets, then we will have to pay a few thousands of SEK for nothing and we really don't have that kind of money Jared."

"Why do you always have to be so damn negative? We'll keep them and that's it, understood?"

"Okay if you say so."

I thought it was a one-time thing but I was so wrong, again. It happened week after week and we lost money every week even if we did win a few small prizes. In the end, we lost a whole lot of money for the organization and had to cover it up with our own money.

GET TOGETHERS WITH ALL OUR MEMBERS

A few months after Jared started his studio, we decided to reward the adult members with an evening round-trip to Denmark to party and get a chance to get to know each other a little more one-on-one. Almost everyone came and we both were very excited. We got on the boat and went straight to the restaurant we were scheduled to be for the night. As soon as the boat left, the bar opened and we all ordered drinks and a few appetizers. We were having a great time, dancing, drinking, giggling, and just having fun, then I saw Emma hand Jared a glass of whiskey and I thought 'Ooh no!' as I walked towards them.

"Jared, please don't drink that. You know you can't handle whiskey and you are always so mean to me when you drink it. Let's just have a good time tonight and remember, these people look up to you."

"Hannah can you just shut up and let me do whatever I want to do."

I turned around for him not to see the tears in my eyes and I went off to the restroom. I got there and looked myself in the mirror while fixing my makeup and thinking to myself, *'Hannah put yourself together now and just pray that Jared won't lose his control tonight in front of these people.'*

Carita came into the restroom and said,

> "Hey girl, this is so much fun. I really needed to get out for a little." She looks at me, "Is everything okay?"

"Yeah, I guess."

"What's going on Hannah?"

"See, Jared cannot handle whiskey very well and he can be kind of mean. Probably not to you guys, but to me, and Emma just gave him a glass."

"Don't worry girl, tonight we are all going to have a good time and Jared won't drink too much. Not now when he is here with us."

I hoped she was right, but no one knows him like I do and especially not these people. When it comes to his karate, Jared always did his best to show a good side. Nothing meant as much to him as his karate studio and everything else that had to do with karate.

When I came back from the restroom, Jared was up dancing with one of the other girls so I sat down with my drink and were talking with the other people at the table. I like these people a lot, they all seemed to be very nice. They knew of course I was Jared's fiancée and the way they were treating me, it showed they liked me too.

After a while, I could see Jared's eyes glazed and he was getting too drunk. I sneaked up to him and whispered in his ear,

> "Jared take it easy with the alcohol, not for me but for you now when everyone is here."

Jared turned his head towards me and I could see his features changing to a drunken phase, as he was getting drunk.

"It's not your fucking business for the hundredth time," he paused and went on, "and if you keeping bugging me, we can talk about it when we get home. I was having a great time until your fat ass started to nag me. Happy now that you killed my good mood?"

He pushed me so I sat down on the couch. Carita saw what happened and came over, took his arm and said,

"Let's go and dance, Jared."

Most probably to get him away from me and I heard her say,

"Don't be like that to Hannah. She is just looking out for you and wants the best for you, Jared."

Later Emma came with another glass of whiskey to him but Carita quickly said,

"No give it to me."

She snapped it from Emma's hand before Jared had a chance to get it. If that had been me, Jared would have slapped my face right there and given me hell when we got home.

My enjoyment for the night was gone now and the only thing left was my fear that Jared would trip out and start to argue with me and call me names in front of his students, maybe even hit me, so I stayed out of his way as much as I could.

Another time, we decided to go out to dinner and partying over on Öckerö with the karate students. We got ready over at Jared's sister Pauli's house, and when we were ready, Pauli dropped us over by the restaurant where we met everybody. We had a great time and a whole bunch of people showed up; even some of the teenagers and their parents came to join us for dinner only. I loved times like this when we all would get together outside the karate studio and just getting to know each other in private.

We believed that friendship and teamwork meant as much as practice to make it a good association. Almost everyone was from here and knew each other somehow, so once we sat down, a whole lot of other people joined us as well. After dinner and dessert, we said goodbye to the young ones and went to a bar close by. The hours passed by and we danced, talked and had a great time all of us, and as so many times before Jared stayed close to Carita all the time even though her boyfriend was there. We left when the place closed and started to walk towards downtown, trying to figure out what we could do so the night didn't have to end yet. This was one of those few times Jared stayed nice the whole night, and we had such a good time that even I had a chance to enjoy myself. We decided that we could have an "after party" at Caritas' and her boyfriend's house.

Millay, my brother's ex-girlfriend, Caritas' boyfriend and I were the first in the crowd to get there but shortly after, we got tired. Millay and I called a cab and went back to Pauli's house to get some sleep; I don't even know what happened to Jared, but he never showed up at Caritas house.

We fell asleep right away, probably because of the alcohol and it was 4:00 a.m. already. I woke up when Jared came in around 6.30 a.m. He was asking me for the car key,

"Why? Where are you going? You're not supposed to drive Jared because you've been drinking."

"Just tell me where the fucking car key is and shut up. It's not your business where I'm going but I'll be back. I forgot my allergy medicine at home if you really need to know!"

Jared left and I lay back down but had a hard time getting back to sleep. I wondered what had happened for him to change like that in the few hours when we "lost" him. Jared acted like Dr. Jekyll and Mr. Hyde, as if he had two personalities and hopefully he would be back to normal when he came back again.

Tim, Pauli's son, came down in the basement around 9.30 a.m. where the guestroom was and looked at us with his innocent blue eyes doing his best to wake us up.

"Can you guys wake up and come play with us up there. Mama said the coffee is ready."

I pulled him to me and gave him a big hug thinking, *'how can I resist this cute little guy,'* and said

"Yeah Tim, we'll be up but give us a minute to wake up okay?"

A big smile in Tim's little face and his eyes were glowing,

"Okay so I'll see you soon," and he ran back up. Millay and I looked at each other and were cracking up.

"What happened to Jared?" Millay asked.

I tried to look secure and calm when I answered

"Jared came around 6.30a.m. but went home for some reason. He'll be back."

I always did my best not to show anyone how much it hurt when Jared acted and did crazy things like that. When he at last came back to pick us up, he had changed clothes and was acting just fine, like nothing ever happened. What I didn't know at this time and would never had found out, if it wasn't for me waking up early in the morning a few weeks later and saw him taking a pill.

I became worried because Jared hadn't told me that there was anything wrong with him. My first thought was, 'is he taking steroids?' That would explain some of his behavior.

"Good morning, Jared. Are you not feeling well? What's wrong?"

"Why do you think something is wrong Hannah?"

Jared snapped at me with an attitude.

"You took a pill and usually you don't like medication at all."

"I didn't take a pill! You're imagination is running wild again."

"Jared, are you taking steroids?"

"What, are you crazy? How dare you even ask me anything like that?"

"Well I just wondered because . . . ."

"Stop being so fucking nosy, mind your own business and if you ever mention anything like that again, I'll give you a lesson you'll never forget. Understood!?"

Jared went to work and I tried to go back to bed and get some more sleep, but it was impossible. I couldn't forget the pill and wondered what kind it was and why he took it, but for my own safety I didn't bring it up again. The answer came a few weeks later when I cleaned out one of our closets and behind the boxes I found a pair of his jeans and underwear.

I got that anxious feeling in my stomach when you just know something is terribly wrong. I picked them up, and there was blood on his underwear and the jeans were covered with grass stains on the knees, just like he was on his knees in grass and had put all his weight on his knees. They were the same clothes he had on the last time we went partying with ISD.

I started to cry when I put one and one together; I knew Jared had been cheating on me. I thought, stupid me, 'This is the reason he had to go home, to change clothes, that time we "lost" him for a few hours.'

All day I was going back and forth in my head how I would take care of this situation and face him with this the best and safest way I could. I knew I had to stay calm when I talked to him, even if it felt like I wanted to explode but of course, that wouldn't help at all; it would just make the situation worse. When I heard the key in the door that afternoon, I still hadn't figured out how to bring it up.

"Hey love, how was your day?" Jared said when I met him in the hallway.

He put his arms around me, leaned forward and gave me a kiss. He felt my taut reaction.

"What's wrong Hannah?"

I released myself from his arms grasp, "Let's talk about it after we are done eating, okay?" I said.

I needed a few more minutes to build up my strength before I confronted him. After dinner, when I put away the dishes, Jared brought it up by saying,

"So what was it you wanted to talk about honey?"

I was standing by the kitchen sink with my back at him but now I turned around and looked straight in his eyes when I asked,

"Please Jared, take this the right way okay, but I need to know. Have you been cheating on me?"

Jared stood up so fast the chair tipped and slid across the floor and hit the wall.

"What the hell! Where did you get that from?"

"I found your jeans and underwear you have been hiding in the closet Jared; the ones with the grass all over them."

I could see Jared was trying to find an answer quick but instead he said,

> "What the fuck was you doing digging in the closet for? You had nothing to do in there."

> "I was trying to organize it to make more space and put away some things when I found it. How come your underwear had blood on them and the jeans grass all over the knees? You wore those clothes when we went out with ISD, that night when you disappeared and didn't come back until the morning with the worse attitude.
> That morning when you said you had to go home and get your medicine, left me and Millay at your sister's while you drove home drunk."

At this point my tears where falling but I continued,

> "You had changed your clothes when you came back, said you had to take a shower because you were so dirty. Did you feel dirty for the reason that you knew you had been cheating on me? Can you please answer my question Jared? I need to know!"

> "First, if I did, no wonder when I have a fat ass bitch as a girlfriend, and second of all, how dare you even ask me something like that? Now come here and do your duty as a wifey. Suck my dick hoe!"

I looked at him through my tears,

> "Are you serious? You've had sex with someone else, been cheating on me and you expect me to satisfy you? How about answers to my questions?"

> "Let me show you how serious I am," Jared said.

He grabbed the back of my neck and pushed me down on my knees in front of him. I looked up at him and continued,

"Was it in this position you did her; whoever it was? That's why you had grass all over your knees?"

Now Jared let go of my neck but instead his fist landed on my ear before he pulled me up, pushed me into the corner and I turned my back against him trying to shield my head from the punches.

"Turn around you little chicken and look at me, see if you want to ask me again?"

He kicked the back of my thigh so I fell down on my knees again.

"Why are you down there, stand up!"

I stood up again but couldn't put any weight on my left leg, it was hurting so much. I turned around just in time to see him unbutton his pants and pull them down, looking at me and pointed down.

"Come here and suck my dick!"

My leg was hurting and my head had already start to get a bump where his fist hit, and there was no chance I could win.
'I better do what he wants.' I limped over to him, looking down at the floor and pleased him while my tears quietly fell, rolling down my cheeks, down my neck and dripped down on the floor.

When Jared came, I got up and walked away to the bathroom without giving him an eye. I could barely breath and took time to give myself a few minutes break from him, dried my eyes, and blew my nose and took a deep breath before I looked myself in the mirror. I hardly recognized myself anymore. My eyes were red from crying and there was no life, they were completely empty. I didn't know how that could be when my heart hurt so much. I was asking myself, *'What was I doing wrong? Have I really been that bad in life to deserve this? Jared's the one who has been cheating on me and he is beating me up? When is all this going to stop? Is it ever going to end?'*

I took another deep breath before I opened the door and had to pass the kitchen where Jared was sitting to get to the bedroom. Neither of us said anything.

I fell asleep quickly, emotionally tired and my body were hurting. I heard when Jared got into bed but kept quiet.

"Hannah wake up."

I pretended to be deeply asleep, but when he tapped my arm, I said,

"What?"

"You must enjoy when I'm beating you up or what's the deal? Why are you always pushing me to the limit Hannah? I don't have any other choice than to teach you how to act. You know I don't want to hurt you, but baby you are making me do it all the time."

"No Jared, of course I don't enjoy it. How can you even ask something stupid like that?"

And now I was wide awake and crying again.

"So why are you always pushing me that far Hannah, if you don't . . ."

"I don't mean to, I'm just saying what's on my mind and my opinion, that's all, and then you are getting mad and act crazy."

"I'm sorry baby, come here," Jared said and pulled me closer to him. "I don't want to hurt you; you know I love you."

That was the last thing I heard before he fell asleep, and I found out later why Jared took the pills; Jared had an STD, Chlamydia.

When Jared blamed it on me by saying that I was the one who cheated and passed it to him, I decided to prove him wrong. I went to the doctor and took all the tests for STD. They all came back negative, but that didn't matter to Jared. It was my fault anyway, and he turned it around saying that I probably had sex with that doctor too.

Time passed by and my emotional life was like a roller coaster, Jared was still abusing me, but not as often as before. There were times when I was sure Jared loved me; then I would lose hope again when Jared either gave me a head bang, a black eye or he almost choked me to death. I could only be happy that I was still alive when that happened.

In early January 1999, I was in the shower and Jared came in, dressed to go to work. He said,

"Hannah, just tell me one thing. How did it feel to fuck Michael?"

I stopped washing my hair and simply looked at him,

"Jared, I have already told you that nothing ever happened between us. We haven't even been working there the last two years, and I haven't talked to any of them at the cab company. Why are you still bringing this up?"

"Listen here hoe! I know what you told me and I don't want to hear it again. This time I want the truth! How did you guys do it? Did Michael get to taste your pussy or did you suck his dick?"

"Jared we were in a club with other people and you can ask them if you don't believe me."

"Why would I believe them? Alex and Nadina, they all licking Michael's ass. Now you tell me what happened. You know I can feel when you're not telling the truth and right now it feels as if I have ants crawling in my entire body."

His voice sounded desperate and Jared came closer to me where I was standing in the bathtub. His eyes turned darker so I knew Jared was losing the control. Scared to death and I didn't know what to do anymore or what to say. He had already made up his mind and it didn't matter what I told him, he wouldn't believe me anyway.

"Yes Jared, I sucked his dick right there on the dance floor." I said trying to make him hear how pathetic it sounded.

Jared suddenly stopped, looked at me with an arrogant smile, and said,

"Now we are getting somewhere. Good girl! Do you see how calm I am when I feel you are telling me the truth?"

I was speechless. *'Now Jared believes me when I'm telling him something so absurd.'*

"Jared, I said that only for you to hear how stupid this whole situation is. I never, ever did anything with him. I wouldn't dare to do anything towards you Jared."

"No you can't take that back. You did suck his dick, I can feel you're telling the truth and you would never lie about anything like that."

"You have been accusing me for years about this Jared, and every time I tell you the truth, that NOTHING happened, but you kept on asking, kept on beating me up for something I never did and I'm so sick of it. Do you know how damn helpless I feel when I'm telling you the truth but you have already made up your mind that I have done something, and now when I'm telling you a lie, you believe me and you know why? Because that's what you *want* to hear Jared!"

He chose to believe a lie rather than the truth.

"Do you think I want my fiancée to go out and suck someone else's dick, bitch? You're more stupid than I thought."

"But Jared, I just told you a lie and now you believe me?" I shook my head, "You better leave before you are late for work," I said.

"Forget about work, I'm going to find out what happened now. Finally you're about to tell the truth how you fucked that taxi fucker that night."

Jared called his work and said "an emergency at home came up" and he can't come in today. When I heard him say that, my body started to shudder and I turned off the water to get out from the bathtub when suddenly Jared is standing in the door again.

"Where do you think you're going?"

"I'm done in the shower and about to get dressed."

"Get back in there taxi fucker."

"But I am done."

"First you lie to me for over two years and now you think you're done?" He smiled and continued, "It just started."

Jared kicked my thigh hard so I fell back in the tub but got up on my feet again as fast as possible and pushed myself up in the corner.

"Please Jared. Stop!"

"Stop Jared," he copied me. "Are you scared now? Were you scared when you sucked his dick too? There is no stop Jared; I have just started. This is just the beginning Hannah."

Since that time when I went out with our co-workers in late 1996 and Jared was sure I had been cheating on him, he had been bringing this up and been beating me up for it many times before. This time was different, I had told Jared exactly what he wanted to hear, and he didn't care if it was a lie.

Jared was the one who had been cheating on me and had a dirty conscience, but now I had given Jared an excuse to turn it around and blame me for cheating on him. He wanted to hear how it happened, when it happened and where it happened. Everything! Now, I didn't have any choice but to expand on the ridiculous lie. More nasty and disgusting for a normal person to believe, but he did. Absolutely unbelievable.

Once in a while, I tried to tell him, it's not true, but those times Jared got even worse so I quit trying, it wasn't worth it. I was desperate and did whatever it took to keep him from beating me, to stay calm, even if it was to build the lie even more. When I told the truth, Jared freaked out, but when I started telling him the nasty lie, he would calm down. It was insane! Every time we argued since that time I went out with our co—workers at the taxi company, when Jared got frustrated, bored, irritated, etc., he brought Michael up. This on top of everything else he found to punish me for, and our fights were horrible.

Jared had now learned to beat me on unexposed places on my body that clothes would cover, so no one would see or suspect what was going on at our house.

ONE OF THOSE TIMES, JULY 1999 CHANGED MY LIFE

We had invited all members of ISD to go to Liseberg, which is the only amusement park in Gothenburg, to have fun and spend the day together. I was excited, every time I went there I would be like a kid again. I used to go on all the rides, but not the new one called "Hangover". The reason was simple, this was an inverted ride, it would stop from time to time without anyone knowing why, in the loop where the wagons would hang upside down, and it could take them hours to get the wagons down. That was enough for me not to get on that ride!

We were a total of fifteen kids and ten adults, and purchased all-day passes which allowed us to ride as many rides as we wanted, and as often as we wanted. I was ready to try out all the rides. The sky was clear blue, the sun was shining and simply a beautiful Swedish summer day, just what we were hoping for. It was so much more fun when the weather was nice than when it was raining.

Jared was actually in a great mood and it gave me hope that this would be a day to remember, and I had no clue how exact I was. Totally unaware of that this day would be the turning point in my life; this day would change my life forever. I got dressed in black flare pants and platform shoes that were extremely high, both at the heel and at the toes so my pants wouldn't drag on the ground.
We were running from one ride to another, to make sure we would not miss any of them. I was giddy with excitement and had a smile on my face the whole day. It had been a long, long time since I was so relaxed and had laughed so much.

Some of the people dropped off after a few hours but we kept on going. Jared and I got everyone together and sat down to have lunch, then we would continue on to the rides we had not yet done.

Jowl, a thirteen year old boy, very tall for his age, wanted to go on the "hang over" ride and asked if Jared could go with him as a kid under sixteen needs an adult to go on some of the rides, and "hang over" was one of them. Jared was not someone who enjoyed the wild rides and Jowl turned towards me,

"Hannah, can you please come with me?"

"No Jowl, I'm not going on that one, but we can go on the one next over from that one."

"Hannah, I don't like that one."

"Okay Jowl, let's make a deal," I said. I couldn't stand when the boy looked so sad; like a sad little puppy, after I had answered no.

"If I go with you on 'hang over' ride, you go with me on the other one," I smiled at him.

Jowl returned the smile, warmly.

"It's a deal Hannah."

We had to wait in line before we could get on the "hangover," and I almost changed my mind a few times, but then I looked at Jowl and saw the excitement in his eyes. It warmed my heart and I just couldn't disappoint him, but I was happy when I could put my feet on the ground again, even though everything went well. I have to admit, it was kind of a rush to be on the "hangover."

Still dizzy from that ride I turned to Jowl,

"Let's go to my ride now Jowl," but the boy shook his head.

"Hannah, I can't do it because the handles squeeze my legs too much."

I gave him a look of disbelief—yeah right! And Jowl immediately said that was indeed the case.

THE EYE-OPENER

Broke my ankle and it saved my life

We had been running around at Liseberg for almost seven hours. Most of the people had dropped off by now but there were still a few of us left and we decided to go to the arcade where the park had most of their games. Jared who was talking to Emma were a few steps ahead of me and Carita when halfway down the stairs, my left knee gave way under me. I sort of slipped down a few steps and then came to rest, and sat down on another step. It didn't hurt, but the problem was that my right foot got stuck somewhere behind me and when I sat down on the step, the foot then came down. I could hear bones breaking but still I didn't feel anything and it didn't hurt.

I figured the sound of bones breaking must just be my imagination, but when it was all the way down, I pulled the leg of my pants up and saw my foot just hanging there, only attached by the skin. I was shocked; it looked like my foot was going to fall off and I knew my ankle was broken. There was nothing supporting my ankle and my foot looked horrible. I started to feel anxious and nauseous. I tried to be brave, I bent down to try to see if I could put the ankle back in place so I wouldn't have to tell Jared, but as soon as I touched my foot the pain hit me and I thought I was going to faint. I knew there was nothing I could do by myself to make it better. It was broken.

Damn! Now is Jared going to be mad at me because I'm so clumsy and had messed up rest of the day for everyone? Before I called his name, I tried one more time to put the foot back in place, at least so it wouldn't look that bad, but there was no chance I could even touch my foot. It was hurting so badly.

Carita was next to me and she saw what happened.

"Hey Jared, wait. Hannah fell and I think she broke her ankle on the stairs."

Now not only was my ankle hurting but my stomach was hurting also and it felt like I was going to vomit. I was worried because the last thing I wanted to deal with was Jared's attitude right now. I knew I messed up the rest of the day but it was an accident and not my fault, but that's not how Jared would see it; accident or not, it would be my fault. He came over and said,

> "Are you sure it is broken Hannah?"

"Yeah, I am," I respond and showed him my ankle.
Jared felt it and I had to bite my lip not to scream. He looked up at me and whispered,

> "What's wrong with you Hannah? Don't you know how to walk no more?"

"Not now Jared when everyone is here," I said with a low voice.

I didn't want Jared to start acting the jerk so his students would hear how he treated me. His students, both adults and kids, looked up so much to him and I wanted that to continue for him. If word got out in Öckerö about Jared's behavior, he would lose his students, and it would be my fault too. I would rather keep things quiet while other people were around. He was about to say something but I cut him off and whispered,

> "Please Jared, not now. I just need to go to the hospital and take care of this, but you can continue here if you want to. I can go by myself."

"Don't be foolish Hannah! You can't even walk correct with two feet so how the hell do you think you can do it with only one? Com' on, let's go towards the entrance and meanwhile I'll call an ambulance."

Before Jared made the call, we collected everyone and told them what had happened and that we had to go. I apologized to them but everyone seemed to be more worried about me. They were very understanding, and I told them I would be fine.

Jared pulled me up and I grabbed the railing by the stairs, tried to walk but I couldn't. The pain was too much and tears came to my eyes as I desperately tried to hold them back. The last thing I need right now is to get more nagging from Jared saying, 'I'm just whining and acting like a cry baby,' so I took a second to dry my cheeks before saying,

"Jared I can't walk on my foot."

He turned around and I thought he was going to slap me, the look in his eyes said that, but he didn't.

"Jump up on my back so I can carry you out."

I did what Jared told me to do and even when I was on his back, for every step Jared took my foot was dangling. Oh my God I was in pain. Fortunately it wasn't too far to the back entrance where we waited no more than five minutes, and I sat on the curb, when the ambulance came.

The ambulance attendant came over and pulled my pants up while he said very nicely and calmly,

"I'm just going to take a look at your foot, okay?"

"Sure."

The ambulance man checked my ankle,

"I know it hurts so I'm going to give you a shot for the pain."
He continued, "I hate this kind of shoes! Those platforms heels can do a whole lot of damage. It looks like they have done it to you."

He asked if I mind if he cut them off me.

"No I don't mind at all. I will never wear shoes like that again so please take them off me."

I think it was between my shock and the shot to relieve the pain that made me relax, so I smiled and was joking around, laughing at my own bad luck. Both ambulance attendants had to put me in the ambulance and one kept me company when we went to the hospital, for safety and making sure I wouldn't faint. Jared followed us by car and I was happy he wasn't in the ambulance with me. It gave me a break from him and I would have a chance to calm my nerves to get the stress level down enough to focus on what the doctor had to tell me about what to do with my ankle.

When we got to the hospital, a nurse put me in a room and almost immediately, the doctor came in.

"I am Jonathan Anderson. So how are you doing today?" he asked while he examined my ankle.

"I'm okay, but I think my ankle could be better."

"Yeah, I think so too. Is this your favorite pair of pants that you are wearing? It will hurt a lot if we pull them off over your ankle, do you mind if I cut them off?"

"Yes it's my favorite pants, but do what you have to do; I have another pair at home."

After Dr. Anderson cut the pants off, he looked at my ankle again and continued,

"Hannah you are going to hate me now but I have to do this as soon as possible."

Just as the doctor finished his sentence, he pulled my foot out and put it back in place before he put a temporary cast on. I looked at him and Dr. Anderson was right, at that very moment, I did hate him as the pain was indescribable!

Another nurse came and took me to get an x-ray and when Dr. Anderson came back to see me, he had a look on his face that I didn't like.

"I have good news and bad news, which one do you want first?"

"Let me hear the bad first," I smiled at him.

"There are three big bones, all of them are broken, and the ligament in the ankle is ripped apart as well. The good news though, they are all clean cuts, not scattered, so it will heal faster and better after the surgery."

I wanted to weep but just asked,

"So when is the surgery, doctor?"

"If there is time, we will do it tomorrow, but latest by the day after."

Early morning the following day, a nice nurse woke me up and said it was time. I was off to surgery and even though it was complicated, it went well and I only had to stay in the hospital for another day before I could go home. I had a cast on my leg, from my foot up to me knee, and was going to have it for six weeks.

Dr. Anderson wanted to talk to both Jared and me, before he let me leave.

"The ankle will heal faster if you're relaxing as much as you can Hannah. No cleaning, doing dishes, laundry or anything like that. Just relax."

"Don't worry doc," Jared said, "I'll take care of everything."

It all sounded good to me, but I was wondering how this was going to turn out. Jared doesn't even make the bed at home.

I called in sick to work and rented a whole lot of movies to watch while Jared was working and took care of his karate students.

The first few days I was enjoying my time off after been running around so much the past fifteen years, but after a while I got restless and bored. Jared didn't do anything at home and I could not see my house fall apart like that. My mother came to help me out with the housework and laundry. Other than that, I spent most of my days alone, watching DVDs and soap operas, but more often I got lost in my own mind; thinking about our wedding, which was coming up in May the following year, and about the future but I thought most about the past.

I thought Jared had changed, he didn't beat me up as much as before. Now when I really thought about it, I realized I was the one who had changed. Jared hadn't change a bit, he had only gotten worse. I had lost myself and didn't know who I was anymore! It happened more often, that I couldn't focus enough on what I was doing, or I got stuck in my own thoughts and where they were going.

I wasn't sure if I was ready to face the truth yet, so to distract myself, I got online and went into one of the chat rooms, and started to talk to people. Soon I realized some of the people there were talking a lot of bullshit! Some were there trying to meet someone, and there were some perverts too, but there were also some real cool people from all over the world and it was so much fun to be able to talk to them. There were a few guys I was chatting with, of course we used false names, but after I had been chatting for a while we exchanged our real names. All of us were from different countries, and when I did run into someone from Sweden, I just stop talking to them, that was too close for comfort.

I was so used to being talked down to and treated like shit by Jared, that now when I was in a normal, pleasant conversation, I was very surprised by this natural mutual respect and I always told them that I had a fiancé. One of those days when Jared and I had a fight, I went chatting online when Jared went to Öckerö.

Marco, a guy from USA, was online and he was happy to see me log on and asked how I was doing. I couldn't even pretend to be okay, so I told him my fiancé and I had been fighting, but I also said something else; I told Marco that Jared was beating me up. I was as surprised as Marco that I told him, because usually I didn't talk about the abuse to anyone. I was the one always finding all kinds of excuses, not to talk about how bad Jared was treating me and why he was doing it.

In the back of my mind and deep in my heart, I knew it was wrong but there was too much fear and I guess I didn't want to see, or I wasn't yet ready to see, how wrong our relationship was. It felt like a stone, or more like a mountain, just fell from my heart as soon as I told Marco. Suddenly I didn't feel so lonely anymore. Marco told me, I deserved so much better. That I deserved a man who would treat me right, and that it was not right what Jared, my fiancé, was doing to me. That there is *never* an excuse to lay a hand on a woman, no matter what! Marco said I should leave him if he doesn't treat me right.

Once again, I was very surprised that Marco actually told me all these things. I mean, instead of just ignoring it, or saying; 'well, it's your own fault if you stay with him, or maybe you deserved it.'

In a strange way, it made me feel better, a little stronger, and when we stopped chatting that evening, I thanked him so much for talking to me and making me feel better. Those feelings I've had inside me for so long, but could never let be known. The ones in the back of my head, started to push again and it gave me headache. I already knew all that stuff Marco told me, but again I had to ignore them for a very long time because I didn't know how to deal with them, and I was too scared to deal with them. I didn't know if I could be strong enough to leave him. But after that night, I couldn't stop thinking about what Marco had said and he made sure not to let me; he brought it up every time we chatted online.

I also communicated online with two other guys, one from Switzerland and one from New Zealand. I told them about my 'Jared situation.' It was such a relief to finally be able, and to dare to share 'my hell' with someone else. It was good for me to get some more feedback and opinions from others. To see if I was totally 'out there', but none of them could believe how someone could be such an insecure man to keep beating up on a woman and especially the woman he claimed to love.

Those chats we had, and everything they said; I just soaked it all up and I started to build my strength and belief in myself again. My online chats with them forced me to see that my situation was so wrong and twisted. Even though I tried to ignore the thought, it would've been easier, but I couldn't. It was there all the time.
Marco and I also exchanged phone numbers and after a while I called him up once, just to speak with him instead of typing. The very first time I heard his voice it was like, wow! Marco sounded so nice. He talked so calmly, which I wasn't used to at all. He only had nice things to say to me. I was used to hearing, most of the time, only negative things about myself—you're so fat, fatso, you're disgusting, a real whore and no one can ever love you. Suddenly to hear these kind things from a man, made a big change in my life.

I know I am a good woman and I deserve to be respected and treated well, just like everyone else. Again, I had thought that Jared changed the last few years as by now, instead of a beating me a few times per week, now it was a few times a month. When I really had the time to think and go over our relationship, I realized one thing, Jared haven't changed at all, it was all on me. I knew when his limit was reached and I didn't push it. I solely did what Jared told me to do, whether I liked it or not.

I also realized Jared would never change or stop beating me, so I had two choices. Either I married him and lived a life of continued torture, in terror, not being able to speak my mind or have my own opinion without being battered; or I had to leave him, but that option wouldn't be easy. If I left him, I would need to leave the country and my family as well to stay alive. I would have to find a way to escape from Jared, he would never let me get out alive, only in a casket. Dead!

Deep inside me, I already had the answer of what to do, but I took my time to let it sink in. It was time to plan how I would escape from him and this nightmare.

Hannah Bonde

After a while, I told my online friends that I had decided to leave my fiancé, and they were happy for me. They said I had made the right decision for myself, and asked where I was planning to go? I didn't know yet, but when I left him, I had to leave the country as well. They wished me the best of luck and told me to stay in touch so they'd know I was okay. I promised to let them know when I, myself knew.

MY FIRST ATTEMPT

September 23, 1999

I woke up at 7:00 a.m. and turned on the computer to check if I got any e-mails. There was only one from Sam, who once again, asked me to let him know where I was going when it was time to leave. I replayed and replayed the thought in my head, and this might sound crazy; but those people I didn't even know, had become my friends and my strength. Somehow, I trusted them because they didn't know Jared, so I told them about my life, and how he abused me, etc. They felt like a lifeline to me. Those online friends helped me open my eyes about my right to have a life, just like everyone else. The saying your home is your castle, that was not true for me; I was a prisoner in my own home.

My biggest fear was for me to be home, as I never knew when Jared was going to be outrageous again. That is why I knew in my mind and in my heart, I had to leave him in order to survive.

I made breakfast and woke him up with a kiss on the cheek and while Jared got in the shower, I started to iron his karate outfit, which always had to be immaculately perfect. When he was done in the shower, it was only for him to put it on before he ate breakfast and I was just on my way to start with the second outfit when Jared sneaked up behind me, pointed to a tiny spot on the first uniform,

> "What is that? Are you always so stupid and filthy when you wash clothes so you can't get them clean? Why don't you use your brain for once and realize there is no way in hell I'm putting a dirty uniform on! Oh that's right, you don't even have a brain!"

> "Jared, I didn't do it, that spot must have came from the washing machine."

I could see Jared was on his way to 'losing it' again, and that would lead to him beating me. He was waiving his hands right in front of my face and I got so scared I closed my eyes, just waiting for the blow to come, but this time I was lucky, it never came. His phone rang.

I thought, today is the day, I just can't do this anymore.

Jared calmed down after he hung up, but the fear and the feeling that there was no one who could help me, still remained. I felt empty inside, as if I was a robot. We ran some errands before it was time for him to leave to his classes at the karate studio and I asked if he could please drop me off downtown where I was supposed to meet my mom for coffee. He agreed and while driving he started to argue again.

"Hannah, why do you never use your brain? I am really starting to believe that the fat in your body has blown your brain out."

Jared had the nastiest attitude, and as he continued to belittle me, I knew my decision was right.

We picked up my mom and Jared was back being the nice, happy son-in-law he thought he would be soon on our upcoming wedding day May 6, 2000. But at that time I would be long gone and far, far away, Jared just didn't knew it yet. Even though my nerves were on edge, I had to act as normal and naturally as I could not to make Jared suspicious. If he did, he would cancel his practice and spend time with my mother and me instead and would ruin my plans.

He dropped us at Café Shiny Day, where mom and I had coffee while I shared my plans with my mother. I mean the plans I had so far.

I was too restless to sit still and told my mom to let us catch the bus home and get this thing started.

Our first stop was at The phone company, to change my cell phone number, which would start off immediately.
"Can you wait and start it like in an hour?"

I tried to buy me some more time but the lady told me it was already done. Damn! If Jared called me now, he would know something was going on, and then he would come home right away. When we got home, I gave my mom a suitcase and told her to pack me some clothes that she know I liked, while I wrote him a letter to explain why I'm leaving. I knew Jared would never understand anyway, but it doesn't matter anymore. *'The only thing that matters from now on, is my life and me.'*

Pressured by the time, mom and I got it done quickly and she called her friend Tom, who came and picked us up. The three of us went back downtown to get something to eat, but I was too agitated and not hungry at all, so while mom and Tom were having dinner, I called my bank and spoke to Larry who's the manager there. He cancelled the connections between Jared's and my accounts and I had all these different feelings in my body. I was afraid; too afraid to put it into words. I was excited as well, thinking of my future. I felt numb and excited at the same time but knew I needed to stay focused at all times. I couldn't afford to relax for even a minute. Finally after all this time, I was on my way to get my life straight. More correct, to get a life!

An hour later, we asked Tom to drop us at the railway station so I could put my bags in a locker instead of carrying them around while I waited for Merissa to come home, so I could go with her. Merissa was a woman I met that same summer in 1999, when I went to a class for people who were preparing to start their own company. Merissa and I connected and I had the courage to open up a little bit more to her regarding Jared's and my relationship, than I had open up to anyone else before. Merissa was my friend, not Jared's, and he just knew her by first name from when I had talked about her.

We sat down on a bench and I looked at my mom, I was exhausted. Finally I'm doing what I should have done years ago; I am taking back my life. My phone had low battery and needed to be charged and I realized that I had messed up, big time. The phone company had given me a piece of paper with my new phone number on, and I had left it on the kitchen table in our apartment. Smart Hannah!

There was only one thing to do, call and change the number again and that's what I did.

Well this time it was the phone company's turn to mess up. Instead of changing the number on my phone, the agent changed the number on Jared's phone. *'Why are things getting messed up, now, when I can least afford it?'* Finally, I got a hold on Merissa so she came down to the station, and the three of us took a cab up to her place.

I remember this like it was yesterday. It was cold and dark with pouring rain outside, and the time had come to say good-bye to my mom. When I looked at her, I saw the sorrow in her eyes and we were both crying.

> "Mama I've got too! Trust me, it will be okay, and I need you to understand one thing. I don't know when, or even if I'll get a chance to talk to you again, but remember to always keep an eye behind you all of the time, in case Jared is trying to come after you to get to me!"

A last hug and my mother got in the cab again. I watched as the car got smaller and smaller. The grief I felt within my heart, was horrible, but I had to focus on me.

> "Bye mom! I love you so much but I don't know when I can see you again; if I ever can see you again," I whispered while the car disappeared.

Up at Merissa's place, she gave me some orange juice and toast.

> "Hannah, you got to eat. You need your energy, girl," and I know Merissa was right.

We were, or most of the time I was, talking until 3:00 a.m. and it was time to get some sleep. I must have been exhausted, because as soon as I lay down, I was out.

September 24, 1999

At 5:00 a.m. my cell phone rang, and when I heard it was Jared, my whole body started to shiver just from hearing his voice. I turned it off and tried to go back to sleep, thinking, *'Jared just have Merissa's first name so it's impossible for him to find me.'* If I only knew how wrong I was!

I slept a few more hours until it was time to get up and call the phone company again to change the number. As soon as I turned my cell back on, Jared called.

"We have to talk Hannah," he said.

"I know, but not right now. I'll call you back," but I knew I wouldn't.

I just needed to get him off the phone, and get some more time to replace the number. I started to shake once again, and I thought it was scary what effect Jared had on me, even if we were only talking on the phone. I finally got everything straightened out with the phone company and got a new number. When Merissa woke up, we ate breakfast and I thanked her again for letting me stay with her, and for being such a good friend. I really appreciated it.

From time to time it felt like I was on my way to falling apart, my legs gave way under me and I had a hard time breathing, but Merissa was there to catch me and pull me right back up. She had to go and buy some groceries and left me alone in her apartment. It was wonderful with the silence and just to be by myself for a while.

When Merissa came back home, I helped to unpack the bags. Knock, knock on the door and with panic in my eyes I looked at her and whispered,

"Do you expect anyone?"

Merissa shook her head, no, and at that moment I knew in my gut who it was. Jared!

I couldn't believe it! It can't be true! But it was.

"I told you Merissa; Jared is the devil, no one can hide from him. He'll never give up, or walk away, so we have to let him in."

My body was shaking like a flag in full wind.

Now, you may wonder why didn't I call the police. Yes, we could have, but I would have, if possible, been in more trouble or even dead, when the police had gotten there.

> "I just want to talk for five minutes and promise I will leave you alone after that," Jared said.

I knew Jared wouldn't leave and to spare Merissa trouble, I started walking towards the door.
> "Stay in the kitchen Merissa and be ready to run out to save yourself, and to call the police, if Jared gets close me, okay?"

My hands were trembling so much when I put them on the handle. I closed my eyes, took a deep breath and opened my eyes again as I unlocked and opened the door.
Once again, I stood face to face with Jared. He looked so sad and I felt pain in my heart, questioning why he was so evil, when he could be sweet as well. *This will be harder than I thought.'* We sat down on the couch and Jared started,

> "I read something at home, and for the first time I realized how bad you have been feeling and how long you've been feeling this way . . ."

Jared was crying, and I didn't know how to handle it when he acted this way. I had never seen Jared so weak, it broke my heart, but I know Jared would never understand what hell he has been putting me through for all this time. All the hurt in my heart and soul, pain in my body and everything else he had been doing for the past fourteen and a half years. He interrupted my thoughts,

> "We can work this out; go to therapy and get the help we both need, but I think we should start by talking, just the two of us."

> "I don't . . . .,"

Jared stopped crying when he cut me short, looked up at me and sounded sincere,

"How about we meet for coffee tomorrow afternoon and start there?"

Before I even had a chance to answer, Jared continued...

"I know it is over between us, and I understand if you never forgive me. I want us to do this the right way Hannah, but I need your help."

If I could help him to get well and get a "normal" life, I would do it. After all, we had spent close to fifteen years together.

"Yeah, we can do that," I said, "but I want my mother to come with me."

"That's okay, I understand."

After I promised to call him and set up a time after talking to my mom, Jared left and I could finally breathe a little easier. I called my mom and she said yes when I asked her to come with me. I also called our friend Lottie to tell her what happened. She told me that Jared had already talked to Gerald, her husband, so they knew I had left, but still Lottie didn't know anything about how very bad our relationship was or the abuse. I never told her anything about it and the reason was that Gerald and Lottie were our mutual friends. Jared is one of their daughter's godfather as well, and the girls love him. I didn't want to ruin his life or anyone's relationship with him, I just wanted to get my own life. Actually to save my life, and stop living in fear all the time. That is the reason why I had to leave.

"Hannah, you know you're always welcome to live here with us. Not as our guest, but to live here."

Lottie interrupted my thoughts, and I responded,

"Thank you so much. You're a really good friend, but no thanks."

I meant every word, but I couldn't move in with them. That would be too much of a risk for their family and me. When Jared gets to that point, he don't hesitate to eliminate everything and anyone in his way, friends or enemies. I have seen it before.
Merissa and I were up talking until early morning again, and after I took a nice hot shower, I fell asleep.

September 25, 1999

I woke up at 9:00 a.m. and called my mom to confirm that she was still coming with me to meet with Jared. Mom said she would be there and we decided to meet at 6:00 p.m. at the mall downtown Gothenburg.

I called to speak to my father when my brother answered and said dad wasn't home. I spoke to John for a few minutes and just before we were going to hang up, he told me he missed me. It brought tears to my eyes and warmed my heart.

> "I miss you too so much. Remember John, even though there is a distance between us, you and your brother are always on my mind and in my heart and I love you. Don't you ever forget that John."

Merissa's mother, Olga, stopped by for an hour and I could see where Merissa got her personality. She was as easy to talk to as Merissa, and I liked her a lot. When it was time for her to leave, she looked at me and wished me good luck with everything, and told me to stay strong. I gave her a smile and said,

"I will do my best."

The day passed by and the later it got, the more nervous I got. I couldn't sit still and I couldn't eat; I was just thinking and analyzed how everything would turn out tonight.
It was time to leave to meet my mom, and together we walked to the place we were going to meet with Jared. I had chosen a restaurant, because I hoped he would behave a little better in public. Jared was already there and though it was cold, he was waiting for us on the patio.

"Do you mind if we sit out here, it is too crowded to talk private in there?" he asks.

"No it's fine, we can sit out here."

"Hannah, I am so sorry for everything I've ever done to you, and I understand if you can't take any more. Still I am begging you, please don't throw away our almost fifteen years together without at least try with a therapist. I know you showed me all signals how bad you were feeling, but I totally ignored it and I am so sorry." He looked down at the table and back up again, "This is so hard Hannah, and we will not solve anything by just sitting here and talking today. It will take time, a long time, and you have to give me that time. You owe me that time Hannah." Jared started to sound desperate, like he was begging me for help. "Can we please go home and talk about things and if you still want to leave after we've talked, I'll let you go. We split our belongings, talk to a therapist to get me well and you can move on with your life."

He was crying now, and it is so difficult to see him so weak and vulnerable. I'm not used to it, but I know he was right. We can't work our relationship out, but maybe at least work things out between us. I mean everything we own is ours and we must be able to talk to each other. I knew it might be a risk to go home with Jared but my belief was that he actually wanted to seek help and getting help was more important.

> "Okay Jared, we can do that. I'll go home with you if you promise me and my mom right here and right now, to never, ever lay your hands on me again."

> "I promise you Hannah, and I promise you Christina, that I won't hurt you ever again. The only thing I want is for us to be happy and to be friends, no matter if it is separate. I know now I need help but I can't do it without you baby."

My mom looked at me and asked if I was sure. I said,

> "No, I'm not, but you know where we live and if you think something is wrong, just call the police and send them over."

We left mom there and went home. I felt kind of, *'maybe we can do this,'* because I know Jared can be calm and talk when he wants to, and if I can help him to get better, I will do it. We came up to the apartment and Jared just locked the bottom lock, put the other keys in our little key-house we had hanging on the wall. Then he said,

> "You can leave whenever you want to."

He smiled at me and behaved well, just as he'd promised my mother.

> "Okay."

We sat down in the kitchen and Jared started out by saying,

> "Thank you for coming home with me and give me another chance. When I first called you and the phone company said the number is disconnected, I thought there must be something wrong. Then when I came home and read the letter you had left, it was as if someone ripped my heart out. First, I got so furious, you can't even imagine, but after a while, I calmed down. I read it again and understood what you were talking about. That's when I realized how I messed things up and I needed to find you so we could talk."

"Jared, how did you get Merissa address? I didn't have it myself."

"Oh that was the easy part. I just called the unemployment office, told them I was interested in hiring Merissa, who went to such and such class, and the lady at the office was happy to help me and gave Merissa's information to me."

That was wrong of the office, but there is nothing we can do about it now, the damage was already done. I thought for myself, *'When Jared wants something, there is nothing that can stop him.'* What's even more scary, is that Jared is smart.
We were talking the whole night about how we were going to do this, who is going to have what and Jared said,

"Hannah, you take the ring, I bought it for you so it is yours."

Once in a while, I got a little scared. It was those times when Jared got irritated, but he calmed down pretty fast. Hours later just when I started to be somewhat more relaxed and comfortable, Jared came with the question that would start the worst week and a half in my life. I would have to fight harder than ever to survive, and one wrong word would kill me! So I really had to be smart and think. I had to be one step ahead of him every single second.

"So baby, tell me about the other guys." Jared said while he turned around, looking at me with a fake smile.

My heart froze and it felt as if someone grabbed me by the neck, trying to choke me when I saw how his eyes changing color, became black and I just then realized what a mistake it was to ever believe him. As calmly as I could, I said,

"You know there are no other guys Jared and there never was anyone else, so please don't go over this again. Remember you promised me and my mom, we're just going to talk and no more fights."

It felt like my stomach was going to turn inside out, but I knew it was no time to be scared; I had to be smart. I was just so tired of everything, all his bullshit, the lies, being abused and never believed, but I had to stay focused and think. It doesn't matter what I say or do anyway, Jared had already made up his mind that I'd been cheating. What made Jared even more dangerous this time; he knew that he had lost the power and control he used to have over my mind and me. I stood up and took a step towards the door and peacefully said,

"I am leaving now, this is not going anywhere."

"You know I don't want to hurt you Hannah, but you make me this way,"

Jared said as he came closer to me. I stepped back, automatically, until I was standing with my back against the wall. With his face only a few inches from my face he continued,

"Leaving? Not in this life time!" Jared made a face that was supposed to be a smile. "Why are you standing all pushed up on the wall you little whore? Are you scared of something?"

He got serious again and dragged me out from the corner by my hair. Once I was out of the corner, he kicked my legs so I fell down on the kitchen floor. He left me there before walking out to the hallway and I heard him go to the door, lock the top lock and take the keys from the key house. Now, there was no chance I could leave, unless I risked the jump from the balcony. It could be worth it if I got a chance even though we lived on the third floor. When Jared came back he sarcastically said,

"Okay now we can talk because you are not going anywhere."

"Jared, you promised my mom and me . . . ."

"What bitch? That I wouldn't beat you up and hurt you no more? Guess what? I lied! Just like you always do."

He stood there looking down at me, grabbed one of the big kitchen knives from the counter and sat down on my stomach. Jared put the knife to my chest and smiled as he said,

"So you little slut, how do you feel now? Want to have some fun first or how about if I make it easy for you? Just stab you like 'ah'," He raised the knife and pretended to stab me. Jared stopped with the knife on my chest again, "You lying bitch!"

I felt the tip of the knife on my chest and I had no more strength to fight him. I gave up!

"Why don't you just do it, so I finally can get some peace?"

But no, Jared wouldn't make it easy for me so he said,

"Why would I do you a favor when you're not doing anything for me but lying, taking all my money and trying to make a fool of me."

I told him to read my diaries if he wanted to know what I have been doing, but he answered,

"No. I don't think so. I'm noble and would never read private things. You probably lied even there just in case I got the idea to read them. How do you think I ever can trust you? You told me you love me and would never leave me, but what did you do? You tried to leave me," he put his head on the side, "but see Miss Piggy, I have already told you; I will find you wherever you are. What is it you don't get Hannah? You are mine forever! That's why, from now on, I have to keep an eye on you 24-7. I will lose so much money because I won't be able to go to work, I have to cancel my karate, I will lose students and money there too. Do you know how much money and time I spent on that karate studio, you fat ass? You'd just love to blow it all for me huh?"

"I know Jared, because I have been here the whole time too and talking about money.... I have put all my money in there too."

"You don't have any money, never had any and never will have any money."

"What about my salaries?"

"That was just money you owe me for being with you, money I spent these years on food, bills, gas etc."

I gave up and kept quiet. It doesn't make sense arguing with Jared. He always comes to his own conclusions, anyway. These fourteen and a half years we've been together he always needed to have power over everything, but there was something he left alone and let me keep private, as far as I know; my journals. That's why I could write in them exactly how I felt; when I was sad or frustrated, or just needed someone to talk to. Sounds crazy, but see, I didn't have anyone to talk to so the journal was my best friend. Not our friend or our thing, it was mine and mine alone.

I know there were people who knew what was going on in our relationship, but they never asked anything. There is a saying "Don't ask if you don't want to hear the truth," and it seemed like no one wanted to hear the truth.

Still holding the knife, Jared pulled me up by my hair and pushed me down on a chair, leaned towards me and pressed the knife so hard into my thigh, I saw my jeans turn red from the blood. Then he suddenly said,

"Let's go to bed."

I thought *'thank you God, it's over,'* but it was far from over. He picked up his black karate belt and told me to lay down close to him while he tied the belt around us. I could feel fear creep over me as I told myself to calm down. *'He will hurt you more if you panic now.'*

"What are you doing Jared, tying the belt around us? And why do you still have your clothes on?"

"Oh and now you try to be a smart bitch?" he said. You left me once and now I need to make sure you won't do another attempt."

"No, but you promised me I could leave if I wanted to."

"Yeah, if you're telling me the truth and don't try to bullshit me as you've been doing all night! Why should I keep my promise, and you can lie your ass off? Do you think it's fun for me to have to raise you? But someone has to teach you how to behave, and what you can and cannot do, when your retarded and stupid parents didn't do a shit."

It was impossible for me to get any sleep, but at least I had a chance to lay down and try to rest the best I could. Rest, so I can keep my focus on how the hell I am going to get out of this situation. I asked myself over and over again, why did I trust and believe him enough to go home with him? The only thing I wanted was to do everything the right way, but it all turned out to be so wrong. He is more dangerous than ever now that he knew he had lost his power over me.

"Jared, you have to untie us because I need to use the restroom."

He looked at me as if he was trying to read my mind, while he released me from his belt. I was on my way to get out of the bed when he said,

"Wait! You're not going nowhere without me." He followed me into the bathroom and while Jared was standing there looking me straight in the eyes, he said,

"See what you have done to me! I can't trust you even to go to the bathroom by yourself anymore. You will try to leave as soon as I take my eyes off of you."

"But Jared, you are the one who has all the keys, so how can I leave?"

"Maybe jump from the balcony, scream for help or who knows, maybe try to kill me. You have a wild mind and never know what kind of idiotic things you can come up with. I don't know what's going on in your mind, bitch!"

No, you're damn right about that,' I thought, *'and I am going to keep it to myself.'* If Jared could have read my mind, I would have been dead!

September 26, 1999 (and the week after)

The whole week was like that! When someone called me, Jared was standing beside me with his ear next to the phone listening to our conversation, and this meant I couldn't ask anyone for help. Instead, I lied and pretended everything was just fine and no one questioned it. Not even my mom or Merissa figured out that things weren't right. He called in sick to work, cancelled most of his karate practice and those few times he didn't, I had to go with him, but he made sure I didn't talk to anyone there. He kept an eye on me all the time. When I went to the bathroom, Jared was there. When I took a shower, Jared was in there watching me etc.

Once I had to go with him to karate practice, he asked,

"Maybe you want to go to my sister Pauli?"

Pauli and her family lived around the corner from his studio.

"Yes I would love to," I said and got my hope up a little.

Jared smiled,
"Too bad but I can't let you go. You would only tell her and ask for help, or maybe you got some of your guys waiting for you so you can get away from me. Sorry you got to wait here."

Why can't he relax for a minute.

"There are no other guys in my life and you know it too."

"Of course there is, and you're probably fucking them all, but let's take that discussion when we get back home."

Over our almost fifteen years together, I have never cheated on Jared. Not once, but he just doesn't believe me. First, I think it is wrong to cheat either when you are dating, in a committed relationship, or married. Second, I would be too scared to do him wrong in any way.

In the car on our way home, Jared started to argue again.

"Hannah, you know I'll stay cool if you're telling me the truth, but when you lie to me, that's when I have to teach you a lesson." He turned his head towards me, "So you were saying you meet him for lunch, at what hotel?"

"I've never done that." I could hear how desperate my voice sounded.

Smack! I didn't expect that punch and my cheek started to hurt badly.

"What did you do that for?"

"Oh you want another one . . . . and you were telling me what hotel you little whore?"

'Here we go again,' I said to myself, and started to make up this story.

I told him I met a guy, who flew in from Switzerland just for three hours to have lunch with me and after we had sex, he flew back. I thought if Jared just heard how pathetic it all sounded, he would understand it is not true, but I was wrong again!

"There you go; now you're telling me the truth. Tell me the details and I want all of it."

"About what?"

"Like room number, which floor, how to get from the elevator to the room and what kind of furniture and decorations were in the room. What position did you use? Did he have a big dick?"

I made some things up and when I was done, Jared said,

"See, it wasn't that bad huh? I am staying peaceful and when we get home, I'm going to call Sheraton and ask about everything you explained for me. If it is as you said; you'll be fine and if not; well then it won't be fun at all, at least not for you," he smiled.

I was still rubbing my cheek, which had swollen and started to turn. I prayed in silence for God to make him realize that I made it all up, and that I had no idea what I was talking about. I asked God to protect me and help me to survive, to help me find a way out of this hell. Either that, or just finish it all so I wouldn't have to suffer anymore.

Once we got home, Jared told me to go straight to the bedroom and from there he called Sheraton to ask about their rooms while he was starring instantly at me. Of course nothing was the way I had told him but instead of realizing I had made it up, now he got that crazy look in his eyes; that look that scares me more than anything else in this world. I was sitting on the bed with my head in my hands and when Jared hung up the phone, I looked up at him.

"Jared, it never happened, why is it so hard for you to believe me? No one is coming from one country to another, just to meet someone for three hours and then go back. And also if it would have happened, how come I didn't leave with that guy in that case. Can't you hear how stupid and insane it all sounds?"

By now I was desperate but he just went on.

"No I can't! And no one would want to have a fatso like you. For fucking? Sure, but bring you back home? Never! And you already know I will find you wherever you go, you can run but you can't hide."

The look in his eyes told me that something terribly bad was about to happen. Jared looked around and walked across the room, grabbed one of my crutches from when I broke my ankle in July, turned around and came towards me as he said,

"Now you fucking whore, Sheraton didn't even have that room number."

He raised the crunches above his head and swung it hard towards my head. I atomically reacted by raising my hands to protect my head and the crunch landed on my left wrist with a big bang. I screamed from the pain, I couldn't help it. It felt like all blood in my arm rushed down to the wrist, and it started to pump so intense, I thought it would explode.

Directly after Jared hit me with the crutch, he threw it to the floor and put his hand over my mouth, and the other arm around my neck. He almost choked me to death and whispered in my ear . . .

"Shut the fuck up before the neighbor calls the police. What is wrong with you? You scream like a pussy as soon as I touch you, but I bet you wasn't screaming when he fucked you huh? Listen now fatso, I told you you're getting hurt if you lie, but I'll kill you if you scream one more time!"

My wrist was swollen, I couldn't move my hand and it hurt so badly I was crying because of the pain. I thought Jared had broken it.

"Just look at you, feeling sorry for yourself, huh? You can only blame yourself, nothing of this would have happened if you were telling me the truth."

He looked down at me and said with a sarcastic smile on his face,

> "That looks really nasty whore, almost like it's broken. I should take you to the doctor and let them take an x-ray of your wrist, but sorry I can't. The hospital will just ask too many questions, like what happen etc. And you can't lie too good. Let me get a bandage and wrap it up for you instead, maybe it will help to heal a little better."

Jared got a bandage and wrapped my wrist, but it was hurting badly. He left the bedroom, and I prayed again to God to help me find a way out before he killed me. When Jared came back, he had a 1.75-liter Smirnoff bottle in his hand and I thought, *'Great, now he's going to drink and get even worse.'*

I by now knew it was going to be a long night, but if I had had any idea of what was coming, I would have preferred that he drank it! Jared stood in front of me,

> "So tell me now Hannah, once and for all, how did he fuck you? Did he fuck you hard, just like the taxi fucker? What position did you guys use? He fucked you in your ass, right? That's why you never let me fuck you there and I have to take it huh? You slut!"

> "Stop it Jared, you know damn well I haven't done anything. Don't you see, even if there would have been an opportunity to be with another guy, I would have been too scared to do it. I know you Jared!"

He just looked at me,

> "You don't know me a shit, bitch."

He took a role of masking tape from his back pocket and started to tape the neck of the Smirnoff bottle. It made me wonder what he was doing and why, but I got the answer soon enough. It was so mortifying and sick and once again it hit me—*I got to get out of here somehow to survive, while I still can.*

"Turn over on your stomach bitch and put your ass up in the air, just the way you did for Mr. Dickhead, right in front of my face."

And so I did, I was too frightened not too.

"Please, Jared please, you really don't want to do this, and if you really look deep inside you, you know I would never do any harm to you."

I heard him laugh behind me.

"I don't know anything deep inside me, other than this little thing," he tapped with his fingers on the bottle, "will be deep inside you very soon."

He held the Smirnoff bottle in one hand and with the other, he grabbed one of my butt cheeks hard and continued,

"So you're not happy with my dick no more huh? It's not good enough for you, must get some bigger and harder. I'll give you some harder and bigger right now you slut."

He forced the taped neck of the bottle in my anus. It was hurting, oh how it was hurting! It felt as if Jared was cutting me with a knife and I automatically and defensively, tensed up as much as possible but it only made it hurt even more. I felt something ran down the inside of my thigh, and when I looked down between my legs, I saw blood.

He is insane, mentally disturbed, crazy and there is no words to describe it! If I survive this night, I need to figure something out and get out of here, somehow. My anus was hurting, and I could feel it all the way inside of me, but there was nothing I could to stop it. I tried my best to be quiet while my tears kept coming. I closed my eyes, trying to think of something else to forget the pain while Jared had his fun at torturing me. Only a sick person with no heart and no compassion for anyone else, could do something that evil.

When Jared thought I had had enough and he his fun he said,

> "Let's get some sleep. You kept me up until 4:00 a.m. with all your bullshit."

He again tied his black belt around us both.

> "Just in case you would get the idea to try to leave. Oops, I forgot, you can't, I got all the keys in my jeans." He slept with his clothes on since that first night and every night. He continued, "I won't take any risks with you."

I closed my eyes and prayed to God, the only one I can talk to without Jared hearing, to help me find a way out of this situation. Alive! I know I couldn't take it much longer, and my tears ran down my face. I tried my best to be quiet so Jared wouldn't hear me crying, as that would make him even madder.

'How did I end up in this situation, but what's even more important right now, how am I getting out of it?'

THE ESCAPE

October 4, 1999

The alarm was going off way too early, I stretched out my hand and turned it off, before I woke him up.

"Jared, can you untie me so I can get up and make us breakfast?"

He did, but got up at the same time, only to sit in the kitchen and watch me prepare the breakfast. Today October 4th, 1999 was my last check up for my ankle, and also the only chance I would have to ask for help. I was praying everything would go well at the doctor today, and even if he said we'd start all over from today, I just couldn't do it. This is not a life. I'm not allowed to talk on the phone, nor walk outside the door by myself. I just live in terror and fear, as a prisoner. I cannot do it any longer.

If Jared would only listen to me when I talked to him, not just hear me, but actually listen what I was telling him. If we would have talked to a therapist as we had agreed to do so he could have gotten the help that he so desperately needed, this week would never have happened and it could have been a reasonably normal separation without all this. That is just commonsense, but I have learned one thing, there is no commonsense with an evil person who is mentally ill.

We ate breakfast before I got in the shower and Jared was standing right there and watched me all time. He had one of those ironic smiles on his face,

"Black and blue is definitely your colors," he said referring to the bruises on my body.

'*How can someone be so obnoxious and coldhearted,*' I thought and felt so frustrated but helpless at the same time. I just wanted to scream, or throw something at him. Just do something to make him SHUT UP! But I didn't. When I was done with my shower, it was Jared's turn and I had to stay in the bathroom where he could see me. It was quiet, no arguments. Thank you God.

On the way to the hospital we were quiet, but inside me I was a wreck. It was around 8.30 a.m. when we got there and Jared sat down while I was going to the cashier's window to announce I was there. The nurse looked up my name and I handled her my free card and ID. I had put a picture of Jared between the free card and my ID, and on the backside of it, I wrote, 'Please help me! Call the police, he is killing me.'

'*Now it is all in their hands and God's hands what's going to happen to me,*' I thought when I sat down again. Soon after, the nurse called my name and showed us to the room where she gave me my papers back smiled and said,

"Oh by the way, a photo was between the papers. It must have slipped in there when you gave me the other papers."

I couldn't believe it! Just could not believe it! None of the nurses read the backside of the photograph. I quickly put everything in my pocket before Jared got the idea to look at them. Just then, Dr. Anderson walked in and told me to sit down while he checked my ankle.

"How does it feel in your ankle, any pain?"

"No, none at all. But from time to time I can feel a little, it can feel a little swollen but it doesn't hurt."

"I think it looks great and the movement is good. So now you don't have to come back for any more check-ups regarding this matter. Do you have any questions or need any more pain pills before I finish this case and let you go home?"

I knew this was my last chance to ask for help. If we went home, either Jared would see what I wrote on the backside of his picture or he would be unhappy with something else. Jared always finds something wrong.

"Yes doc there is one thing, can I talk to you in private for a minute?"

"Sure," Dr. Anderson said and turned his head towards Jared, "Can you please excuse us for a minute?"

Not a word from Jared and I stared down on the floor, scared to death of looking at his face, but I could feel him trying to force me to look at him. Jared knew as well as I did, if I looked at him, he would have the power again and I would change my mind. I would be too scared and too weak to follow through, to take it all the way, so I just kept on looking down on his shoes as Jared slowly backed out of the room. The whole atmosphere was tense with frustration. Jared knew what was coming and that I was going to ask for help. He didn't want to get caught, so he most likely would leave now when he knew I was about to ask for help. As soon as Jared left the room and the door closed, I told the doctor,

"Please help me, he's killing me. Look," I said and took the bandage off my wrist, it was still a little swollen and bruised. "He hit me with my crutches. He has kicked me and been beating me up the past week and a half. He kept me a prisoner in the house." I pulled my pants down to show him my bruised hips and back. I pulled my shirt up to show him my chest, all black and blue from the abuse. "If you don't help me now, Jared will kill me as soon as we get in the car or when we get home."

I saw how shocked Dr. Anderson was and he didn't say a word at first, but he checked my wrist and I whispered with tears in my eyes,

"Please help me."

"First it needs to be x-rayed and after that we will figure something out for you," he responded with serious voice.

Dr. Anderson opened the door and I thought Jared had been scared and left, but I was mistaken. He was still there, sitting right outside in the hallway waiting for us to come out. I immediately started to feel how I was losing strength, and the weakness was coming back. I repeated for myself that if I didn't do this now, I would be dead, so I followed Dr. Anderson when he passed Jared and the doctor said,

> "We need to take her up for an x-ray of her wrist," but before Dr. Anderson could get beyond the door, Jared got up, grabbed my jacket and started to run while he pulled me along with him.

> "It's not over yet bitch."

'It is now or never! If Jared pulls me out with him, I will never get out of this alive.' I just screamed and took all my strength and stopped.

> Fortunately, his hand slipped off my jacket so I could turn around and run back towards the doctor. I thought he would try to come after me again, but he kept on running out through the doors.

> Nurses came running and asked if I was okay. I shook my head and started to cry. I just felt so weak and so hurt but at the same time relieved. He still had my purse and my right shoe since I had to take it off to get my ankle checked, but it didn't matter. At least I was alive.

> "Take her to another room in case Jared tries to come back and find her, and I want you to stay with her, until we know how to handle this situation," Dr. Anderson told one of the nurses.

While the nurse walked me to another room she said,

> "I am so sorry; you guys have looked like the happiest and cutest couple who have been in here the whole summer. We had no idea."

> "I know. Jared can fool anyone."

> The nurse asked a number of questions including how long Jared had been abusing me and as I relayed my story, I was crying. So

much hurt and so much pain, but I was happy to be alive. I had to call my mom to let her know what had happened just in case Jared got the idea to try to get to her. After almost fifteen years with him, I know how his mind works, and as he often said, "If you can't get to the person you want, there is always people close to them you can get, and it will hurt just as much."

Hospital security came to take me over to Emergency, and to be safer, we walked through the basement where only the staff are allowed. At the ER, another nurse took x-rays, and pictures of all the bruises on my body, while someone else drew some picture diagrams of where the injuries were and how they looked.

I was black and blue all over my body on areas that couldn't be seen when I was dressed. Jared was cunning enough to hit me on those places where the bruises wouldn't be visible. That way, there would be no questions about what happened.

Susanne, one of the nurses, called Merissa and asked if she could come down here and keep me company, and she said she would be down as soon as possible.

A therapist came in to talk with me and when Merissa came, I told her everything that happened. She said she knew something was wrong when we spoke by phone, but she didn't know what to do, and said she was so very sorry.

This whole thing is so absurd, I don't know if I'm going to laugh or cry—maybe both. Cry for all the years I was so miserable and laugh because I came out from my hell still alive. The whole situation is just sick and outrageous, so unbelievable that my life would turn out this way.

I talked to my sister Annie by phone and she told me dad was in the hospital in Spain, and this time he was in critical condition. Who knows if my father will ever come back home? His health is not good at all and it seems as if his lifestyle and all that alcohol have gotten to him and his liver. Everything seems to happen at the same time. When it rains, it pours.

Another doctor told me they needed additional x-rays, so back to x-ray. The nurses informed me they wanted to make sure they collected all the evidence and documentation, if I decide to press charges against him. Someone was by my side all the time, for which I was very grateful. They gave me something to eat and my mom showed up after she was done working. My mother's eyes were red from the crying and when she saw my body, I thought mom was going to faint. She just about fell apart.

"Oh my little angel, what did Jared do to you?" she cried.

I started to cry again and hugged her.

"Mama it is okay. I'm alive and I'm never going back to him."

One of the nurses had talked to a safe house and the manager there said I was welcome to come. Security came and took me down to where they keep all transportation for the hospital. It was in one of their vehicles that would take me to the safe house—a women's shelter. Only God knows what was going to happen with me now, but I knew for sure, everything would be better than with Jared.

I hugged and kissed my mom and once again, it was time for a good-bye, but this time it was different. From now on, I was on the run, and I know Jared would do everything and anything in his power to find me.

"Mom, listen to me real good now. I want you, Patrick and Annie to be careful when you're out in public, at home or everywhere. Always keep an eye over your shoulder and always know that Jared could be somewhere close by. Don't ever under estimate him. He's smart and if he can't find me, he might want to get to you, only to make me come out from wherever I'm hiding."

"I will be careful and whatever you do my little angel, don't let him get to you."

Merissa could travel to the women shelter with me and on the way there I looked at her and asked, somewhat to myself as well—

"Why did it have to come to this? This is not what I wanted. I just wanted us to go our separate ways and each have a happy life. It just didn't work for us together! Now I have to be on the run from him. For how long? Is this going to be for the rest of my life?"

She didn't say nothing as there was no answer. I was exhausted when we got there, and the manager was a nice woman named Alita, she was waiting at the door to welcome me. Alita made us some coffee while she told me the rules and how everything worked there. I got my own room but I needed to buy my own food, shampoo and incidentals. I didn't have any money or anything, just the clothes I was wearing and only one shoe, but Alita was nice and brought me a little food so I at least could have some breakfast in the morning. I could use public phone on the premises up until the staff left to go home for the day and I called my sister and Liza, my dad's wife.

My sister Annie knew what had happened so I told Liza also, and asked her to tell my dad when she felt that he would be strong enough to hear. Both told me to press charges against him, but I didn't know. I couldn't decide. I was confused. If I did, Jared would lose his license to teach karate, his studio and *maybe* he would get a few months in jail if I were lucky. After that, Jared would think he really has a reason to destroy me, to eliminate me.

So far, the only thing I had done was to leave him, without any harm to him or his life. I don't know if it made any difference to him, but I thought *'better safe than sorry.'*
It was 9.40 p.m. and my first night at this place, my new place—a women's shelter. All the staff had gone home, and it was just me and two other ladies there, but I stayed in my room the rest of the night.

SHELTERED

October 5, 1999

I didn't sleep well at all last night, I was way too anxious. The other lady, Beth who works there, was in the office so I said hello to her.

"Hi and welcome," she smiled at me, "Come on in and tell me why a young lady like you are here."

I told her a little about my life and in particular, the latest happenings.

"I am so happy you got the strength to leave."
I took a second and answered,

"Yeah, I am too."

I called my mom to see if she was okay. She was happy to hear from me and to hear my voice. She had told her boss about what had happened to me, just in case Jared should come by her office and try to start trouble with her. I told her that if he called and asked about me, that she should tell him that I am at a place where I get some rest and have peace of mind. My mother was also going to drop off my stepfather's cell phone and some money with Merissa for her to bring them to me.

"I really appreciate it mom, thank you."

I called the phone company to change my phone number, *again*, and order a new SIM card, they could send it to where I was staying. I also called my bank to block my VISA card and of course, Jared had already taken all the money he could get out from the ATM. I knew that he would so I wasn't surprised.

The bank manager, Larry, with whom I had been doing business, was going to send me another card. He offered to transfer my funds via phone, a wire transfer, so I wouldn't have to go to the bank.

"Thanks, that would be great."

'I am so blessed to have these people in my life at this very moment,' I thought to myself.

Last night I wrote a letter to Jared explaining why I left him again. I thought that maybe Jared would understand me better and let go of me. I also put a brochure in the envelope about an organization that helps men who can't control themselves, men who are abusive and/or mentally ill.

Alita and Beth said it was a bad idea to write to him, but I thought it was important for him to get help, and I wanted him to have the information. I guess I was still hoping Jared would save himself by getting some help. I promised them both that they didn't have to worry about me going back to him. It would never happen. **Not ever**!

When Alita left that day, I gave her the letter and asked her to mail it for me. She was hesitating at first but agreed to. In the meantime, I was worrying about money and called Dr. Anderson to see if he could extend my time off from work, so I wouldn't need to start drawing unemployment money, at least not just yet. It went to his voicemail so I would have to try again tomorrow.

I was anxious to get my cell phone and the new number. I ran water in the bathtub so I could take a hot bath; maybe that would help me to relax a little. I got undressed and when I passed the mirror, I got a huge shock.

"God damn Hannah, look at your body," I said aloud. "How did you allow your life to turn out this way?"

My entire body was aching and I could see the pain in my eyes—that was a pain from my heart and soul coming from being abused and hurt for such a long time. Such a long time, that I had lost myself and all hope for a future. It wasn't pleasant, but as they say—the truth hurts. *'No point in looking back. Just think of your future now.'*

The strange thing is I'm not sad, just frustrated, scared and also excited; excited to be alive, to start my new life, and to make my own decisions, glad that I never again have to live in constant fear. Never to be beaten, again! I had the freedom to decide what to do, and where to go, and I am free to speak up for myself. It felt wonderful!

My life will be so different from now on, but even though it is really nice and comfortable here where I am staying, I still need to figure out what I want to do with my life. The cost is $20 a day to stay here and I can't afford it, but I will find a way to work it out somehow. I don't have any other choice at this very moment.

I felt tired and confused. Hopefully, I will get a good rest tonight as I need all my strength and energy.

October 6, 1999

I was even more tired when I woke up than when I went to bed the night before. My arm and chest hurt so terribly and I was very fearful. My mind started to analyze again; *'what if Jared shows up one day and finds me here? What if he'*—I stopped myself and asked, *'how could he? Places like this are not listed in the phonebook and only Merissa knows where I am.'*

Yesterday when I looked out my window I could see my sister and Ploppen, her pit bull, go for a walk and I started to sob. I missed them, I missed being in touch and wanted to say hi, but it was better for all of us if no one knew where I was.
I got up to make some coffee and asked Inga, one of the other ladies here, if she wanted some. She said, yes and asked if she could help? When the coffee was ready, we sat down and talked. I asked her about her situation and Inga told me it was the third time she is there.

"My husband is an alcoholic, and sometimes when he drinks, he gets violent," but Inga won't divorce him. She continued, "Hannah, I am older, but you have your whole life in front of you. Whatever you do, don't go back to him. Don't be a fool like me."

"Don't worry, I will never go back."

When Beth came that day, I called Dr. Anderson, but still couldn't get a hold of him, so I left my number again hoping he would return my call. I called Lottie also, just to let her know what had happened, and to tell her I left Jared for sure this time and that I was safe. I promised her to keep them updated on what was happening with me. Lottie and Gerald still didn't know how dreadful it really was, how terrible Jared had been treating me.

After that, I pulled out the Yellow Pages and called different airlines to get the price of a ticket to California. The best I could find, was a ticket valid for three months costing $875 with a choice of dates, beginning late October or beginning November. Besides that, I would need a tourist VISA, a new passport and driver's license, right now I didn't have anything, not even my ID. All of those things were either at home or in my purse, which Jared had, but I had no chance of him giving them to me. I started to feel desperate and wondered how I was going to get all these things accomplished. I started the self-talk again; I had to try to remain calm and not panic, after all, that wouldn't help.

I took a shower. My hand was in a lot of pain today. Damn it! When I got dressed, I saw a little bird sitting outside my window looking at me. It was as if the little bird was trying to tell me something—'you are free as a bird now, spread your wings and fly away Hannah.'

When the bird flew away, I felt a little better, and I knew what I had to do. I need to fly away, just like the bird just did. Someone knocked at my door.

"Come in."

"Do you want to come and have a cup of coffee with us out here?"

It was one of the volunteer girls who used to come here on Wednesdays to keep us company.

"I'd love to, give me a sec and I'll be out."

I could definitely use some company and let my mind rest from all the stress.
In the beginning, I was only listening and observing, I didn't say much. Anne who was Eva's daughter, started to talk to me and after a few minutes, I was fully engaged in the conversation and excited. Anne was going to give me some clothes, we were both about the same size, and I really needed some. When the volunteer girls left, they all gave me hugs and kisses, and wished me well.

Merissa finally called, and she told me Jared was harassing her and had now finally dropped my shoe off at her place with a letter for me. I told her to put the letter in the trash, I didn't want it. I needed to be strong by myself, and Jared needed to let go of me and realize I didn't want to deal with him anymore.
I told Merissa that if Jared kept harassing her she should call the police, unfortunately I couldn't do anything about it.

I watched a show called *"To Have And To Hold,"* and my mind automatically went to our planned wedding day, May 6, 2000, but it will never happen! Thank God!
Even though I felt a little safer at the women's shelter, I always locked the door to my room at night. One thing for sure, I am not going to make it easy for him to get to me, but I'm sure Jared is trying to plan and scheme in his head right now. Trying to figure out; where I am and what or how he can find me. The people here at the woman's shelter, asked if I wanted them to go with me and get some things from my house, but I said no. The only way for me to get any of my things would be if the police come with me, but Jared would never open the door, so leave well enough alone.

It's 10.30 p.m., time for me to go to bed. I was thinking about all the happy days waiting for me in California, closed my eyes and fell asleep.

October 7, 1999

I was expecting or anticipating a good night's sleep last night, but I was wrong. I was more anxious than ever, and woke up in the middle of the night screaming. I thought Jared was in the apartment on his way into my room. There was no way I could go back to sleep so I listened to music and tried to relax.

In the morning when I heard someone else was up, I unlocked the door to my room and went out. Ingrid and Alita were in the kitchen making breakfast. They asked if I wanted some? but I said "No thank you, just a cup of coffee." I don't eat much these days, but no wonder, huh? I make sure to drink enough liquid as that is most important for now. I know everyone is worried about me, but I'm doing fine here.

I just need to organize everything before I leave; get a travel Visa, a passport and identification. I don't even know how long I will stay in California. I might stay in one city for a while, and then move on somewhere else, or I might stay forever in the first city. It all depends and only time will tell. One thing is for sure though; I will never ever tolerate a man who abuses me, either mentally or physically.

'Never again!'

The only passport I could get in short order was an emergency, temporary passport, valid only for three months. This means, I would only get a tourist Visa for three months. *'Oh well! I just need to get out of Sweden and off to another country. I will worry about those issues later.'*

I thought of calling Jared to see if I could get some of my things with help from the police, it was the only option and if not—I guess I would have to start all over, including buying clothes.

'Wonder where I will be, and what I will do for the millennium.' The thoughts flew through my mind. As of right now, I don't have a clue. What I do know, is that I appreciate everybody who helped me so much with everything. I was amazed that people were so very helpful to little, tiny me.

Alita was going to the store so I gave her my last money to get some groceries for me, then I got in the bathtub. Today I am very anxious, and maybe a bath will help me to calm down. The bath water was running and I called my mom to see how she was doing. I looked at myself in the mirror and today, my hand was even more bruised, and it hurts all the way into my soul. *'An abused woman in the mirror and that woman is me.'* This was the first time I truly admit to myself and now realized I was one of those many abused women. I had never before looked at myself and used the word "abused". I've always said Jared was hitting me and beating me up, but now I had opened my eyes and be honest to myself, even though it was painful. I was an abused woman! With that consciousness, my determination became deeper and stronger when I again looked at the abused woman in the mirror. It's incredibly hard to believe that woman is me. I looked straight into my eyes and said

'Get a life Hannah, get a life!'

That is exactly what I intend to do! My self-talk continued:

'You deserve a nice, quiet life. A life filled with happiness, good people and lots of love.'

Could it possibly be worse than what I have already been through? That someone trying and wants to kill me?

I would love to find a man who respects me and loves me for who I am. A man who treats me lovingly and with trust, but first it's time for me to take care of myself and heal. Heal both my body and soul, so I can be that strong woman I truly know I am. For now, I just need to keep thinking that there is no one but me, and no one who can tell me what to do or when to do it. I have the power over my own thoughts and mind, it's all on me.

I must have dozed off in the bathtub, so I got up, dried myself and went into my room. I put on some music and lay down in my bed, tossing and turning, trying to get some sleep, but I was still so scared

Jared was going to find me. *'I don't want to go back. I can't go back and I am not going back, not under any condition!'*

Alita knocked at the door and asked if I wanted to come and keep them company out on the balcony?

"Sure I'll be there."

Honestly, I don't really like to be out there. What if Jared would pass and somehow see me? I would die!

I hadn't got the SIM card from the phone company, so I called them again to see what the holdup was. Their answer, "We sent it to you October 5th, so you should have gotten it today. If you don't have it by tomorrow just call us back." Well at least I have a pre-paid phone card for now, but I still feel limited.

I think I will call Jared next week about picking up some clothes, but what if he followed the police back here? I don't want him to know where I am staying.
I was restless so I vacuumed and mopped the floors, cleaned the bathroom to burn off nervous energy. The place looked much better now.

"You want some of my soup Hannah?" Inga asked.

"Yeah, I haven't had anything to eat all day."

We talked about our problems, but figured out it was better to forget about the men. I think that is a great idea! I went to bed early and my phone was ringing in the middle of the night; it was Anna and we talked for a while. She told me she would be able to meet Merissa next week to get my shoe. It will be good to have both shoes when it is time for me to leave here.

October 8, 1999

When I woke up, I thought it was 8.30 a.m., but it was only 7.30 a.m. I tried calling Merissa but her phone was off. I guess she thought it was Jared who had called her 500 times yesterday, but it was I and I felt sad for dragging her into this situation—I am so sorry Merissa.

I got up, read the newspaper, and felt a little depressed today. Maybe I would feel better if I had some of my own stuff, but it is what it is and I just have to get accustomed to it. I'm thinking too much. Sometimes when people don't answer the phone, I feel like no one wants to deal with me and that everything I bring is drama, and I feel so lonely. I know it's not normal of me to think like that, but these thoughts come to me.

Finally, I got a hold on Dr. Anderson today and I thanked him for all his help on Monday. He informed me that the nurses had been upset and scared for the situation, but what matters was that I am doing well and was safe. He was also going to extend my sick benefit for another month, and that's better than nothing. I don't even know how long I will stay here at this place or when it will be time for me to leave.

When Alita came up, she had a few things for me in the mail. I got my new ATM card today and now only the pin was missing before I can use it. I also called the phone company to check with them regarding my sim-card, but the reason I didn't get it, was because they had messed up. I could not believe it, but they had sent it to Grevegardsvagen, my old address where Jared lived and now I was told that they'd send me a new one without any cost to me. There was also a letter from my mom and I started to shed tears like a baby. It wasn't sad, but very emotional. My mother told me Jared was going to see a therapist at the Men's Crisis Center today and wanted me to call him. I think it will be good for him, but we will never get back together. If I had any feelings left for Jared when I left the first time, he completely killed them all, when he nearly took my life that last week, abusing me both the physically and verbally. He just can't understand the damage he has actually done to me, not only physical and mental damage to my life, but damaging his as well.

Inga and I become close friends, and it was nice to have someone to talk to; and someone who actually knew what I was talking about and who was in the same situation.

We didn't do much, just watched TV the rest of the night. My wrist didn't look good at all. It is swollen, bruised and still hurt badly, but sooner or later it would heal, just like I would. I have to stay positive.

Liza called to tell me Jared had contacted her in Spain but she told him that no one in my family didn't want to have anything to do with him anymore. I was glad my father and Liza did what they felt was right for them, and of course that they supported me. I can't focus and don't have the energy to focus on what everyone else does, I need to focus on what I have to do.

When I call Jared next week we'll see what happens. At least he knew I had not pressed charges against him so maybe he would spare me—I can always hope.

October 9, 1999

At 8:00 a.m. I opened my blue eyes but stayed in bed, listening to the radio until 10.30 a.m. I got up, put on the coffee maker for us, and called Lottie. She told me her brother Richard was coming to dinner, and I am more than welcome too.

"Thank you, but no thank you. Can I take a rain check?"

"How about if the kids and I come and visit with you where you are today?"

I hesitated at first but knew it would be good for me so I said,

"Why not," and I told her where I was.

While I waited for them to show up, I tried to call Merissa again and to my surprise, she answered.

"Jared has been calling me non-stop and accusing me for lying to him about you."

Once again, I felt so bad for putting her in this position.

"I am so sorry girl," but Merissa said it was ok.

Inga was out smoking on the balcony and I went out to keep her company. Oh it would be good to smoke a cigarette now, but I knew better than to fall for the temptation.

I jumped in the shower and washed my hair before Lottie and the girls came, the least I can do is to feel nice and smell good when my three girls get here. Anna called at the same time as they walked in the door, but I said I'd call her back. It was so good to see them and the girls hugged me so hard. Still I didn't feel like I could talk to Lottie and tell everything, as I had been telling Merissa as her family are Jared's friend as well. Lottie asked if I wanted to come with them to McDonalds in Kungsbacka instead, but I declined. It would have been so much easier if she knew everything, but I'm not going to tell her. Her husband Gerald called while they were still here and told her, that I could come and live with them whenever I wanted to. It warmed my heart even though I knew I would never accept their offer.

Before they left, Lottie started to talk about the argument Jared and I had at the Christmas party, about that time he went out to dinner with another girl. Lottie told me that our co-workers had been upset with him because they loved me. I was Line Express Bus' little sunshine and they didn't want to see me get hurt. That was the reason everyone at the company disliked Jared before we stopped working there.

When it was time for them to leave, around 3:00 p.m., Lottie told me they weren't pleased to hear about me moving out of the country.

"Maybe I'd find a man and get married, and then you guys would come and visit me."

Lottie didn't think they would be able to afford such a trip. We were playing around with that thought for a minute and laughed out loud, before we said good-bye.

I was in a better mood than I had been in a long time. I thought about what Lottie had said, and I couldn't wait to start my new life, my own life! It's going to be fantastic!

After dinner with Eva and Inga, we watched Top Gun on TV, but it was too romantic for me and I went into my room and started to write again.

When I write, it is like therapy for me. I get my emotions out and it makes me more determined and stronger. I will not let anyone come between my friends and me again, no one. The only thing that can end our friendship is if the person tells me him/herself that he/she don't want to deal with me anymore. I went to bed around 12:00 midnight but I probably didn't fall asleep until I think it was closer to 1:00 a.m.

October 10, 1999

It was almost 10:00 a.m. when I woke up and I already knew today was going be a difficult day. I wrote a poem to Merissa and a letter to send her, as I think she is going through a hard time now. That is probably why she doesn't answer her phone. I am feeling restless and lonely.

I got up at 10.45 am, put on some coffee, and called my dad to ask if he could call me back. I wanted to talk to my father but my phone card was close to fully spent. Of course, he would call back.

"How are you Hannah?"

I could hear in his voice how worried he was about me. I told him everything was fine, or as good as it could be under the circumstances. My father didn't feel well himself, and I didn't want to make it worse for him by revealing how bad it had been.

Dad said Jared called yesterday but I didn't even ask what he wanted, I really don't care. We hung up and it was time for breakfast, but again, I didn't have any appetite so I just poured myself a cup of coffee. My phone went off and it was Lottie, she told me Jared called them again and she had told him how disappointed they were with him after seeing my hands. Jared had responded,

"What did she tell you?"

"She didn't say anything, until I asked her straight out. Then Hannah told me what had happen. Would she have lied to me right to my face?"

"Nah, I guess not. Hannah trusts you."

Jared also had told her to ask me if I could call him, 'just really quick,' regarding one thing that his therapist asked him. Lottie said she would, but with no promises that I would call back. He also told them that if I moved in with them, he gives his word not to bother me there, but all Jared wanted was for me to come out from wherever I was hiding, so it was too big a risk for all of us. I don't trust him and never will! I found out he was now seeing the therapist Mondays, Wednesdays and Fridays.

Lottie said something that caused me to wonder; she begged me not to tell him it was completely over, because she had told him I hadn't made any decisions yet. I tried to call him a few times after when we hung up, but there was no answer. *'Jared is probably out teaching his classes in Öckerö. I will try later.'* Now I felt strong enough to talk to him on the phone, and maybe we could end all this bullshit for the last time. I feel it deep down inside, all I want, is for this to end.

Anna came over and I read some of my poems I've been writing for her. She liked them a lot and commented that,

"In all this darkness, you still see a light at the end of the tunnel, huh? That is awesome, and you will have a wonderful life Hannah."

I am excited to start a new life filled with possibilities even if it scares me too. That is something so unknown for me, but everything has a first time. I can get my own life and I can eventually figure out whom I am, not what someone else wants me to be, but whom I am! I really wish that Jared would realize soon that he has a life even without me and just leave me alone. I hope he gets the help he so desperately needs. Then he can meet another girl and have a wonderful, a normal life.

From now on, I will make all my decisions as to what I want, and trust myself without asking for other people's opinion all the time. If I decide to go to California, than I buy a ticket and tell my parents and friends I'm taking off. Of course, my friends will miss me, I will miss them too, but I will keep in touch with them.

All day I was watching TV and Lottie called at 4.30 p.m. to tell me Jared had called again to say if I could call him at 6:00 p.m. when he gets home from karate.
Also, Jared might have been upset since I let her see my bruised hands but I really don't care anymore. Yes, I was so careful before, not to let anyone see how badly Jared was treating me, but it is over now, at least I didn't call the police on him. Not yet anyway. I don't wish Jared any ill, I just want my own life. If we can work this situation out without drama it would be so nice, but he really needs to stop trying to control me. I have had enough!

If he just stays relaxed and calm for now, I will be happy, but he has told me so many times before, he will never forget. Staying calm even for now is good. I just need some time to get my life on the right track again. Maybe with the passage of time and his visits with the therapist, Jared will let me go.

It was now 6:00 p.m. and I was nervous while dialing his number. Jared answered after the first ring and while we were talking, I became calmer. He told me he had been talking to a therapist and he said,

"After all you've been through you need to do the same. I am worried about you."

"There is no need to, everything is fine with me."

Jared couldn't understand why I hadn't talked to the police when I claimed I was so scared he would find me.

"I don't want any difficulty or harm to come to you in any way Jared, and I don't want you to lose your karate studio. That's why."

He wanted us to meet face to face and talk. I said we could do that but only under one condition; that we do it at his therapist's office and I would have someone from here with me. That was fine but then after that, we needed to work out our personal things, just him and me, he said. I couldn't believe what I was hearing. Jared still didn't understand that I am serious this time. Once again, I explained to him that we never are going to live together again and we will never get back together.

"Is there someone else?"

"No there is not!"

I knew it is useless to try to make Jared understand something he doesn't *want* to understand. I told him I was thinking about picking up some of my things with a police escort and as I expected, he exploded. He said I didn't need to exaggerate so much.

"I suggest you reconsider that decision and start to act like a grown woman, eh?"

I thought to myself, *'which of us here doesn't know how to act normal?'* Yeah, this shows how different our minds work.

If Jared brings clothes and the things I need to the therapist on Wednesday, we don't have to worry about all this with the police. He agreed and said it was okay with him, he would bring them.

When we hung up, I had mixed feelings. I felt good about the situation, me talking to him, but I said what I wanted and I was not under his control anymore. On the other hand, it was hopeless because I couldn't, no one could make him understand.

I have come so much further than he has in processing our individual situation. Jared still cannot believe or accept that he has lost power over my mind and me. Additionally, I am so much stronger than Jared is physically, and even after all the bullshit he put me through, Jared still has a whole lot to work out with himself. There is no way I would meet with him alone one more time.

I told Inga what Jared said and she asked me what we are going to do with our joint financial responsibilities. I told her if we can meet and do this together with other people in a peaceful atmosphere, then all would be fine, but if Jared insisted on doing it the two of us alone, then I will just forget about the whole thing. I will pack my bags and leave. I would not try to fix our finances and pay with my life. There is no way I would take that risk!

Do I sound selfish? Maybe I am, but that's the way it has to be. If Jared doesn't want to solve this with other people around, then it won't get solved at all.

I am so determined now and I will not change my mind. Call me a coward, or that I don't know responsibility, but I don't care. People can call me whatever and say whatever they want to say about me. What matters is how I feel and to save my life. If you think I should be ashamed, too bad but this is it for me.

I tried to get hold of Merissa again but her phone was still turned off. If she doesn't want to deal with me and my problems, why doesn't she just tell me, instead of staying away. Merissa was supposed to stop by today, but she didn't call or show up.

I went to bed around 10.45 p.m. and the weekend was over. Tomorrow is Monday and I was happy about a new week. This weekend has been so long. Before I fall asleep, I whispered, good night my family and friends, sweet dreams to you.

October 11, 1999

'*I can't breathe, help me,*' that was the first thing on my mind and I woke up. I looked around and when I realized where I was, I took a deep breath and started to cry when the panic attack was over. It was just a dream. I was dreaming that Jared forced me to go with him and sleep at home again, the house we both occupied back then. When I calmed down and my breathing was back to normal, I could now think somewhat rationally—'*no one can ever force me to go back there again, no one in the whole wide world.*' That filled me with a nice feeling.

8.55 a.m. I woke up again, and it was time to get up. Beth was there, and I asked if I could talk to her when she had the time.

"Sure let us talk now Hannah."

We had a coffee and I told her about the conversation I had with Jared yesterday, and asked if she could come with me on Wednesday.

"Sure I'll do, but before that I need some guarantees from his therapist. To meet with him, we need a security to be there all the time, and also that his therapist is not going to try to convince you to solve this situation alone."

After my bath I finally got a hold on Merissa and she apologized for being unavailable. I asked her to let me know if she didn't want to talk with me anymore, but just don't leave me wondering. She said she would never do anything like that to me, that she would always keep it honest.

She is coming to visit me tomorrow and I look forward to seeing her again. It has been a week and I really miss her. It would be so much fun if Merissa would come with me when I leave, but I don't think she will. She means a lot to me and her mom had told her to be here for me, which she has been.

She has also been through a similar situation and knows the ups and downs, ins and outs of the situation I was in. When she needed a friend and shoulder there was no one there, and that is why she wants to be here for me.

I had promised to call Jared again today and it was getting close to 3:00 p.m. I started to feel anxious, but I called anyway. I had promised him. Our conversation went reasonably well, but we had some difference of opinions about certain things. What I want is the most important thing for me now, but Jared still tried to tell me what to do and how I should feel.

I spoke to my mom before I called Lottie and asked if Jared could drop my things off at their house? Maybe she could bring them over here? She said he already had dropped it off there. So many people involved now and honestly, I'm wondering how this thriller is going to end.

If I notice one little thing, such as Jared trying to get to me, I'm taking off. I am out of there! I just need to get another passport, as soon as I get my new driver's license of course. I won't tell Jared anything about my plans for the future. I had already started my new life without him, and that's how I'm going to continue my life.

Beth and Inga came back after going over to pick up some clothes at Inga's house, and we sat down for a coffee and talked. Yeah I know, there is a whole lot of coffee and talking, but we really don't have anything else to do when we have to stay in all day, every day.

Again, Beth brought up pressing charges against Jared, for the reason that most likely he will do the same thing to the next girl he meets.

"I would, if I knew the police would put Jared in jail, and that someone could protect me, but the laws here in Sweden are a joke. You know as well as I do, there might not even be a trial. The judge might just write it off, even with all the evidence. In that case I'm dead, Beth."

I know these people want what is best for me, but I know Jared. And right now, I have not really messed anything up for him to be able to continue his life. I am not strong enough yet to even think of someone else but myself. And that is hard enough.

Alita brought some new dishes over to the apartment and gave me the responsibility to organize everything. It was nice to get full trust and responsibility for something. I went to bed around 10.30 p.m. and started to feel sick in my throat again. Sore throat and runny nose is the last thing I need, but hopefully it feels better tomorrow after some sleep. Like every other night, I whispered good night my family and friends. *'Even if I don't talk to all of you right now, I hope you know you're always in my heart.'*

October 12, 1999

Last night was another night when I couldn't sleep at all, this time because my nose was running all night and I was coughing. I don't need this now!

I started to think about where I wanted to go when I would leave and it just seemed like my mind is set on California. My cousin Lynn lives in New York and it would make more sense to go there, but I want California, so more likely that will be my destination. I can't help but wonder if Jared and I are going to work out our situation, but I have a funny feeling in my stomach, it hurts just thinking about it. That is not a good sign.

I got up at 8.45 a.m. made some coffee, and right when it was ready, Beth and Alex (her son) showed up. They had their little dog with them, and he was the cutest little thing.

I called the unemployment office to see how much I owed them and told them I would pay them as soon I got my money. I can't risk being kicked out from here.

Alex and I were listening to music and it was funny, despite the age difference, we like the same kind of music.

At 1:00 p.m., it was soap opera time on TV, *Days Of Our Lives* and Alex watched it too. I don't think he does normally, because that's the time he's in school.

I cleaned up in the kitchen and Anne, the therapist with whom I have been talking, called me. It was nice to talk to her, as always, and I got an appointment with her on Tuesday at 9:00 a.m. I am very glad.

I called Jared and I don't know why I did, as it stresses me so much every time I talk to him. I know Jared can't do me anything by talking on the phone, so there is no reason to be stressed, but I am. It's his birthday on Friday and he asked if my mom and I wanted to go out to dinner with him this weekend, for the last time. I didn't give him an answer. It felt like Jared was choking me just by asking. He cannot possibly be aware of what damage he has done to me. If he were, Jared would never have asked me to even call him from the very beginning. I asked him if he had told his older sister Pauli that it is over between us, but he said no.

"You should, so they don't have to wonder why we never come out and visit anymore. The kids adore you Jared."

I said I was going to call him Thursday, but he asked if I could please call tomorrow, 'so he could get a chance to hear my voice.' I don't even know why, but of course I said yes. Somehow, it feels as if Jared still partly controls me. It is scary.

When we hung up, I got this panic attack again and I started to cry. I don't want to do what Jared is telling or asking me. It is as Jared still manages my mind and I cannot say no to him. I telephoned my mom for some comfort and she asked if I wanted her to come and visit me.

"Yeah, I would love to see you mom."

Beth held me in her arms until I stopped crying, and my stomach felt better, it was not as tense as before. I watched TV until my mom came and it was so wonderful to see her again. Last time was at the hospital when all this had just happen. We hugged for a long time and then I gave her a house tour. Inga and my mom had a cigarette on the balcony while I was in the kitchen making some coffee and snacks for us. Inga left us alone so we could talk, and I told my mom

> "I want to show you what my body looks like, and explain what Jared did to me."

My mother didn't want to see, she refused to see, but I told her anyway how my hand turned out this way. How Jared was swinging my crunches towards my head, and I raised my hand to protect my head. I wanted her to know how really life-threatening it was for me, and maybe then my mother would understand what a hell I'd been through. She couldn't stay as long as I wanted, but we got a little time together to talk. The last thing my mom said before she left was,

> "What if you didn't put your hand up to protect your head, you would have been dead now."

"Yes mom, I would have."

I think this is the first time my mother realized how serious this abuse was and has been all these years. She had seen me bruised and swollen, and with both eyes black and blue, but I think this time my mother really understood it. It's a shame it took such a long time.

When I went to bed at 11.15 p.m. I felt so sad and blank inside, in my soul. I hope that tomorrow I feel better.

October 13, 1999

Not even a good night sleep helped, I was still coughing and my nose was totally stopped up. Good timing huh! I wrote a letter to my sister and while I was writing, I got sad and started to cry again, as so many times before when I remembered my past.

At 10.30 a.m. I was ready to go out to the others and have some coffee, but no one had made any, so I did. My phone rang and it was Lottie. She said Jared had just called her and asked if she could call me, to tell me to call him, and I said okay. She warned me that Jared sounded very strange in his voice and manner. I called him and without saying hello or anything, Jared asked me if I was in Spain.

"No I'm in Sweden."

He asked for a number to call me, just to confirm I was telling the truth and if I did, then he would believe and trust me.

"No you won't Jared, but why would I go to Spain?"

He was in Spain he said and there was panic in his voice.

"What the hell are you doing in Spain?"

He must be totally out of control.

"I want to talk to you Hannah and I thought you went down here to your dad. Do you know that your father is in the hospital again?"

"Yes I do know that."

Don't ask me why I did what I did. I don't know why and cannot explain why I did it, but I gave him the number to the pay phone we have here and told him he could just use that number now and I will answer just to prove to him that I'm telling him the truth.

He called, and got so surprised and sounded so much calmer when I did answer the phone.

'Why do I let him play with my mind like this? I don't know, but I guess it is a very bad habit I've got. Only I can stop this mind game that Jared is playing with me.'

What make someone so desperate, that he would take a car trip all the way to Spain, only to see if I were at my dad's house? Jared really wants to control me totally, 100%, and panics when he cannot.

Come on get a life, is all I can say! No one is ever going to control me like that again.

We talked for a long time and I told him straight out how hard it is for me to talk to him and how I feel stressed and anxious just thinking about talking to him. I don't know if I'm going to laugh or cry anymore. I'm just emotionally drained.

Beth came up and had some mail for me. One was a note from the Frolunda Police Department, where it said they got a tip from someone who told them about the abuse. Damn it, I don't want to get the police involved. Jared is going to think I am the one who called them. I called the police and told the officer, Ivar Back, that I didn't want to press charges. I just wanted to get my own life.

"You know Hannah, only that Jared tied you up will put him in jail. That is kidnapping."

"See, you can't guarantee it, and that's why I'm not going to do it. I'm not playing with my life like that."

Detective Ivar said he wanted to come and talk to me in person and I said okay, but I won't change my mind. I suddenly got this horrible headache. Of course, it was caused by stress. I don't think there is a chance for me to have a normal life if Jared knew or found out that I put him behind bars. If I put him there, then I know for sure that I won't get out of this alive. Oh my head is killing me!

Fortunately I'm on the sick list until October 31. Then I will try to find another doctor who can extend it for me, even if I will be out the country. I need to get all the money I can, from everywhere and for as long as I can, because I don't know when I'll get a job over there. I called my mom and asked if she could come and keep me company tomorrow.

"Maybe I can have a sleepover with you?" she asked.

"That would be so nice."

Two of those volunteer girls came up and as usual, I was the one talking the most, but it must be that I need it the most. When they left, I tried to reach Merissa and she was over at her mom's house. I told her about the crazy thing Jared had done, and Merissa was shocked.

"Wow! Jared really wants to find you girl, no doubt about that."

We decided that Merissa would come up here tomorrow and drop of my shoe and the letter from Jared. Now we knew it was safe because Jared was out of the country.

I got tired and went to bed at 10:00 p.m., but woke up when Jared called at 12:00 a.m. After we've been talking just a minute, he started to threaten me by saying,

"If you don't work this out with me Hannah, and just take off somewhere, this is going to end really drastic and bad. It's not a threat Hannah, just a statement. Also, what did you get that idea from that I kept you locked up as a prisoner at home and slept with my clothes on so I could hold on to our keys at night?
Why are you telling all these lies about me? So have you talked to the other guys, your other boyfriends?"

Now I got pissed off, it wasn't funny!

"It's not your business anymore, Jared! I can talk to whom I want and when I want."

Jared didn't like that at all and kept going, but I didn't care at this point. He went on,

"So now you're going to act like a hardheaded three-year old kid, huh? And why don't you keep your phone on at night, busy with something?"

I told him that I can turn off my phone whenever I want to, and how frustrated it makes me when he is still trying to control me like that.

Honestly, after this talk I don't think we EVER are going to solve this issue. Just when I had that thought, Jared said,

"You can call your boyfriends when you feel down, so now you can do me the favor and have the last birthday dinner with me right."

I never thought about this before but Jared is excessively unstable for me to even consider meeting with him. I was tired and told him I'd call him tomorrow at 10:00 a.m. to talk some more and he said,

"Yeah, you better do. You know a person can be 'mentally confused' from time to time and go off and hurt someone, stabbing a person you care for with a knife or something like that by mistake."

That is if I did something or just left without letting him know of course! And Jared wants and expects me to trust him. No way!

Jared is right when he says we actually have had some good memories too and not just bad ones, but the good ones can't cover up for the bad ones anymore. Also, I had never left him before, not like this time and Jared was fully aware of that. The power he once had over me was fading and as I said before, now it's all about survival for me. I would rather stop communications with everyone around me and with him if that were what it takes. I will change my cell phone number again and move too. One thing is for sure, I'm going to come out of this alive.

He just doesn't understand! He is pushing me further and further away every time he makes certain comments or threats like that. What is wrong with that man?

It's 2:00 a.m. now and I'm not even tired, just tired of someone trying to take my life.

October 14, 1999

I woke up at 9.30 a.m. and I was still tired. I believe I'm emotionally drained, I definitely have the flu and I sound like I am losing my voice. Why is this happening to me?
I got up to make myself some breakfast but I wasn't hungry so I changed my mind. I am much too anxious. Jared called me and said he has been talking to Lottie again. She had told him I was about to leave the country. I didn't respond. He started to talk about his birthday again.

I don't know why he doesn't get it. I don't want to and I'm too scared to see him again. I'm not going to see him. We hung up and I was going to take a bath. Jared called again and was telling me,

"Don't you dare just leave without helping me first! We are going to work out everything between us. Do you understand that! There is no other choice."

I hung up on him. I cannot stand the effect he has on me. After my bath, Beth asked if she could talk to me alone. We went downstairs to the rec room, and I told her exactly how I feel about all this. She was worried about what is going to happen with me. We talked for about two hours and in the interim, Jared called five times. The last time he called, Beth answered and told him to stop calling. Right! As if he was going to listen to her.

I was tired of talking to him, so I called the phone company and changed my number once again, but Jared could still terrorize us by calling on the payphone. He is going to explode when he can't reach me anymore, but it was necessary for me to stop the communication. This is the only way I can stay calm and start my healing process. Then Jared won't be able to influence me and twist my mind, but now he just keeps pushing it and playing with my mind.

I'm going to tell everyone, I don't want to hear if Jared calls, if he asks them to tell me to call or whatever he says. I don't want to hear anything that has to do with him!

Simply, I can't. I just can't, if I am ever going to heal.

My sister Annie came up for coffee. She had a flower for me, and it's always nice to have some company. I'm glad that she and I have become closer to each other than we were before. She was the one who hated Jared most of everyone.

I was so upset with Lottie and couldn't get it out of my mind that she told Jared my plans. I called her up to ask how and why she did something like that, especially because she knew all that was going on and Lottie told me Jared had threatened her. He told her that if I moved to another country, he would put the blame on her even if it wasn't her doing. Either way, I'm not going to change my mind.

Wow! What can I say? Jared was now threatening our friends. Lottie asked for the name and number of the police officer I talked to earlier and I gave her the officer's information.

Ten minutes after we hung up, Officer Ivar Back called me and said he wouldn't have time to see me at the station Tuesday and asked if he could come by here instead. God I am so tired of all this. I feel sorry now. This will shut down his karate studio when The Swedish Budo organization hears about this. Damn Jared!

The charges will destroy his livelihood; his life will be in pieces, and just another reason to be furious at me. For every negative thing that happens in his life, the more rage will be built and the more dangerous he will become, and he will make sure I'll be the one to pay for it.

My therapist called me and it is comforting to talk to her, even though it's just on the phone.

My mom came up for a sleepover and she brought some delicious cookies. I ate a few, as the only thing I had to eat today was a sandwich that Inga insisted that I ate.
It was so wonderful to have mom here so we could sit up and talk. I told her how tough and more unsafe it was now that the police are involved. Mom was going to talk to my sister and see if Annie could withdraw the charges against him. Annie was the one who had told the police about everything.

It was nice and quiet now when my phone didn't ring constantly, and it was less stressful for me when I didn't have to talk to Jared.

I washed a load of laundry for us and I was getting tired so afterwards it was time for bed. My mind was very active, and I was thinking too much. I had to say to myself—'stop thinking now Hannah and take everything day by day. You need your rest so you can get the energy and strength you need.'

Good night everyone.

October 15, 1999

Inga knocked at my door to wake me up at 9.30 a.m. I did not sleep well at all last night. It's Jared's birthday today, and that is probably why. It is going to be his first birthday in 15 years that we don't celebrate together. It feels somewhat sad. Actually just the fact that all this has happened is sad.

Once again, I started to cry because I felt sad for him having to celebrate his birthday by himself, so I asked my mom if she would call Pauli and please ask her and the family to support him as much as they can. I know Jared would never ask for help, and he doesn't even realize that he need someone to emotionally support him.

Why do I even care when I need to focus on taking care of myself?

Inga said it is because I still have feelings for him, but I don't know if it's that, or if it's that I feel sorry for him. I just know whatever it is, I need to get over it now, because Jared and I will never be together again. There is no 'we' anymore, only me now!

Because it would only take one more time for him to see me—it just takes one time to kill me.

I needed to make some telephone calls to apply for my new driver's license. It would probably take about two weeks before I would get it, and after that, I would get my new passport, probably also in two weeks, and with my new documents, I would be good to go.

Officer Ivar Back had talked to Alita and he will be here on Monday, at 2.25 p.m. to talk to me. Beth said the officer wants to discuss everything from the very beginning, but I really do not want to talk to him at all. If the police wants to continue these charges they can go ahead, but do not involve me in it more. I'm the one in danger and I have to live as if I am a hunted animal, not them! I'm the one who would pay with my life.

One thing that I am so tired of is people telling me that—you have to do this and you have to do that; press charges here and let Jared get what he deserves.

I am tired of people telling me what to do. I know they mean well, but no one knows Jared like me and they don't know what he is capable of.

I don't want to talk to him, I can't any more, but I want to say Happy Birthday, so I called ISD's answer machine and left a message. Of course I started to weep, but at least I said Happy Birthday.

I felt a little better after taking my shower. I actually ate some real food today, instead of just a sandwich. Before I left him the first time, my weight was almost 190 lbs, in just three weeks I had lost 13 lbs. I was too unwell and anxious to eat.

My mom called at 5:00 p.m. to tell me that Jared had called her and told her to thank me for calling him. My mother continued with when she asked where he was, his response sounded weird.

Now I am anxious again, and I am thinking Jared would find out where I was, and come over here. I hate that feeling! *'Before I go to bed tonight, I have to check that all doors are locked.'*

I was writing a whole lot today and I feel incredibly restless and abandoned by everyone, so I am happy Inga was here.
She always went to bed early but I was still up, thinking about when I'll leave for California. I will probably celebrate both Christmas and New Year there, somewhere. I might be alone, but at least I will be free.

Beth told me before she left, that if I move out of the country, that she will come and visit me. I know my life will be so different from What it has been up to now, and only God knows what the universe has in store for me and what my destiny is.

I went to bed at 1:00 a.m. I was so tired.

October 16, 1999

I woke up at 9.30 a.m. but stayed in bed until 10:00 a.m. Today is my nephew Jay's fourteenth birthday, and it makes me sad because I cannot call him. It's Saturday and I don't like the weekends here, the time goes so slowly. I'm feeling like some kind of prisoner here too, because the only thing I can do is to stay in the apartment. I cannot go out. I know it is temporary and what is best for me, and there are some positive things too. The most positive is that no one is beating me up here.

I called my mom while I was making breakfast because I needed to talk to her regarding all this with the police charges and stuff. If Jared gets arrested, then it would mess up my plans too. I would have to be here for the trial and all the responsibility about the apartment and our other bills would be on me. I need to have as much money as possible when I leave, and it was costing me room and board every day here too. My sister called and asked if she could come visit me. Annie came up with Ploppen, and she brought a photo album for me, which I truly appreciated. Even though her life is messed up with too much drug use, my sister was still there for me now when I need her.

After Annie left, I finish watching Jurassic Park just to give my mind a break. I am thinking way too much.

Later that night, when Inga and I were sitting on the balcony talking, it was around 10:00 p.m. I saw Jared pulling into the parking lot. I thought my heart stop beating.

Inga tried to convince me that Jared cannot see me up here but I was scared to death anyway. With fear in my voice I said,

"You don't know what Jared is capable of."

I called Lottie and her husband Gerald, to distract myself and get my mind on something else. Inga went to bed before me but I just couldn't relax yet so I sat up writing in my journal.

I also wrote three new poems. It's a way for me to express my feelings. The fear I feel when I see him is more powerful than words can explain. Once again, I was reminded of how frightened I am of him. I would never go back to him. Maybe, hopefully, I will never ever see him face to face again.

I was sure Jared would show up in the hallway, and I was sitting with my phone ready to dial 911. Everyone keeps telling me Jared is not "Spiderman," and I know that, but they don't know what he is capable of, and they don't know Jared the way I do.

At 2:00 a.m., I was exhausted and went to my room, locked the door and lay down with my cell phone in my hand, just in case.

October 17, 1999

I woke up at 10:00 a.m. and was so surprised that I had slept well all night. I got my coffee and tried to get a hold on my mother but couldn't. I really needed to talk to her about the police report against Jared. It stresses me even more and my sister has to drop the charges for me. I don't want anything, anything at all to mess up my plans, but I know her, she won't!

I felt panic. I started to vacuum the place, and mop the floor, when my mom showed up and it was an excuse for me to take a break. I explained it all to her until she got the point and decided to talk to Annie as soon as she had a chance. I really would appreciate and be relieved if mom convinced her to drop the charges. When I called mom later that night to see what Annie said, mom told me Jared had visited her.

"What!"

Jared has absolutely crossed the line and this whole situation is out of control. He told her that now it was all up to me; that if I refused to solve this without any damage to his life, he would get himself a studio in jail. What Jared meant was that he had nothing to lose by killing me. He would have a roof over his head, food to eat and could get an education, so thinking about it, jail in Sweden was not that bad. I got so irritated and wrote some more poems before it was bedtime at 12.30 a.m.

Why can't Jared just leave my family and me alone and get a life of his own?

October 18, 1999

Inga was banging on my door and said it's time to get up. I was so tired but I had to get up anyway, otherwise I would be late to my meeting with Anne, the therapist with whom I have spoken by telephone a couple of times. Today is my first time to actually meet

with her. I had a quick coffee and then took the elevator down to the parking lot where Alita had her car. In some strange way, I didn't feel scared thinking that Jared could show up, but I know I have a weakness if he would and when he is sad.
I know how to handle Jared when he is mad and aggressive, but I do not have a clue what to do when he is crying and showing weakness. Jared wants me to give the two of us another chance but I can't. If I did, I would let myself down, and I cannot do that one more time. Been there, done that too many times already.

It was nice to be around people again. This is the first time since I came to the women's shelter, even though I kept a cautious eye out at all times. We got to the hospital and when it was my turn, I didn't know where to start, but once I started it all came tumbling out. I broke down in tears a few times and it was hard to talk about all this because it hurts so much.

While I'm sitting here writing my tears are falling. It's as if I see my whole life in slow motion and from the outside for the very first time. It hurts in my heart and soul to see how I've been living; the fear, the controlling behavior and the mental and physical abuse.

I cannot believe I didn't stop this a long time ago. Maybe it would have been easier if it came in small doses, little by little, but now I got it all at once. No wonder I felt so stressed and anxious. I got sick and I was losing my hair.

When I was talking to Anne, it was about my entire life. Even things in my childhood came up, and when I left an hour and a half later, I felt a little better. It was not easy to talk about the heavy burden I had as a kid, and the pain as an adult, but it was good to get it out.

After my visit to the therapist, I asked Alita if we could stop at the mall because I needed to get some things and we did. I got myself some new makeup as I wanted to show my best side on my passport picture. Officer Ivar Back came on time and Alita put us in a room where we could talk without being disturbed.

"So Ms. Bonde, do you want to tell me what happened? How come a young lady like you are here?"

I told him why and continued saying that I'm not going to press charges against Jared. Officer Back told me, as so many others already had, that even if I get away, Jared will do the same thing to the next girl that he meets.

"Officer, the only thing I want is to have my own life, a quiet and peaceful life. Is that too much to ask for?"

"No Hannah, it's not, and you deserve it. But can't you . . . ."

"No I can't Ivar, I need to think of myself first. What if I did it, can you guarantee that you can protect me and that Jared will go to jail?"

"Well if there is enough evidence, we can get him."

"But you can't guarantee it, so I'm not doing it."

Officer Back did his very best to make me change my mind, but I didn't. If I decide to press charges and put Jared behind bars, he would get me for sure.

"With a good lawyer Jared would be out in no time. I can't take that risk."

"Okay Hannah, if you change your mind, you have my number. I am out of cards but will send you one as soon as possible. You can save another girl out there from going through the same thing you have."

"My main concern and priority is to save myself."
Ivar Back was very nice and said right before he left,

"While you were talking to me, I thought of a song that fits your situation . . ."

"Which one?" I asked.

"When I send you my card, I will tell you."

Officer Back smiled at me and even though I know he was frustrated with me for not signing the papers, it seemed as if he understood my way of thinking, and respected that.

When he left, I called some different cell phone stores to see how much it was to buy a phone that would work in the US. It would be so nice to have one, but at the same time, I needed all the cash I could get so maybe it would be better to buy one when I get to my destination. I was worrying how am I going to survive economically and I don't know how expensive it is to live there, but no, I can't worry about it now. First, I need somewhere to stay when I arrive and then take it day by day.

'It will be ok. I will be ok.'

I called my mom and Jared had been there to drop off some of my things. Finally!

Right now it just feels like I need to leave as soon as possible, otherwise something or someone is going to try to stop me. But I'm telling you . . . . *NOTHING* is going to stop me this time.

October 19, 1999

I woke up at 9.45 a.m. and went to the kitchen and made some coffee. It seems like I'm tired all the time, but I know what it is. I am emotionally drained, and it will take all my energy to stay strong and listen to my inner voice. Not Jared's or anyone else's around me.

I didn't do too much today other than fantasying about how wonderful my new life will be but I also struggled with a lot of feelings.

October 20, 1999

It was just 7:00 a.m. when I woke up but I didn't want to get up at all. I was tossing and turning, trying to get some more sleep, but I gave it up at 8.15 a.m. Inga was surprised but happy to see me up early and we had breakfast together. Alita came up with our newspaper GP; she had been here since 6.30 a.m.

When we were done with breakfast, I got on the phone and called the US embassy to see how I could obtain a US Visa. I had no clue, because I had never been outside Europe. Okay this was the deal, you can stay in the US for 90 days with the tourist Visa you'll get when you enter the country, but you must apply for a tourist Visa before you leave, if you are planning to stay longer than 90 days. Well 90 days is nothing, and if you apply for a tourist Visa, you need a good reason and it's the immigration authority who decides yes or no. Is saving my life reason enough for them? Why does it have to be so complicated?

Hopefully, the doctor can get me a paper that I can be out of the country but still be on the sick list. In one way or another, I have to work this out really soon.
My sister came up carrying the suitcase with clothes that Jared dropped off at my mother's and I was happy to finally get some of my own clothes. Jared had also put a card in there to me, and the poem brought me to tears. And even though Jared had been treating me so badly, it is still hard to go through and deal with this.

Ilana came to cut Inga's hair and afterwards when they were done, we all had coffee and talked. She was so kind and I told her my story and my plans for my future. She understood, because that was exactly the same way she felt when she left Iran and moved to Sweden and finally a new life. Ilana is happy now; has a wonderful life and a husband who love her and treats her very well. She assured me that that is what I was going to find in California, too. Now I was more convinced than ever that I had to leave. Her visit today meant so much to me, more than any of us knew.

My mom showed up to say hello, and I told her how I felt regarding Lottie and her husband. It feels as if it's necessary to cut off everything from my old life to be able to start my new life, at least from now until I leave.

I will continue to keep in touch with the people I met here at the women's shelter as good as I can. All of them belong in my new life, the very beginning of my new life.

My mother thinks Lottie will understand if I tell her I need time, and maybe she will. It is nice to have my mother to talk to now, but at the same time, I have to wonder. I mean, I know my mother likes Jared too even if I am her daughter and she should have my back. I honestly don't think my mother truly understands me, or maybe she does deep, deep inside, and she knows what needs to be done, but if that is the case, my mother ignores that feeling completely.

I got a chance to talk deep today and when Ilana left, she gave me a hug and whispered to me—your time is now Hannah. Those words gave me so much strength and made me even more determined than I was before.

As soon as my mom came home, she called me again and asked me to call Jared, so I did. Stupid me!

Jared asked me if I liked the card and I said, "yes I did, but it made me cry." He said he missed me so much and that he can't live without me. I told him that I had already made my decision but he refused to accept it. He just kept talking as if he was ignoring everything I said. Suddenly Jared asked if I intended to solve everything around us, and I told him,

"Yes, of course."

"In that case, I want to see you in person. Face to face Hannah.
I have to."

I told him I'm not ready to see him, and he continued,

> "Well the bills won't wait until your Hare Krishna foolishness is over. The people you have around you these days are telling you what to do and not to give me one more chance. Those words are not yours Hannah. I know you love me. Those people pack your head with all that bullshit, don't you see?"

I just thought to myself, Wow! The way Jared is talking tells me that he definitely doesn't know me anymore. I ran out of money on my calling card and promised him to call back when I had put some more on it, but it was a promise I wouldn't keep, I didn't have the strength to keep.

I cannot talk to him anymore. Jared is draining me more than ever and I cannot take it. He will never understand and realize what he has done to me. He twists every word and now I felt like the bad one. Just because I broke that promise to call him back, and I didn't. I talked to Inga about it.

> "Why am I still calling him and trying to work it out in a good way when I know it won't work?"

> "I don't know darling, I don't know."

Inga was happy today because her husband had finally signed all the divorce papers and I was happy for her. She is a very nice lady and what I like about her, is that she has never judged me. Not once! Inga went to bed at 11.30 p.m. and then it was my 'me time'. Somehow, I started to feel stressed and anxious. I needed to vent, so I called an emergency number for women who need to talk to someone. I talked to the lady for 30 minutes and then I didn't have any more money, but it was worth every penny.

I went to bed at 1.30 a.m. and I was so tired. I was lucky, I didn't know before what damage Jared would do, and if I did, I would have been too scared and probably never left him at all.

October 21, 1999

I woke up at 8:00 a.m. and as usual I didn't want to get up, but of course I did. My mind was working, analyzing things too much for me to go back to sleep. It feels like I can't get my thoughts straight; I keep on forgetting things or maybe it is because I have too much on my mind. I'm just staying here all day, every day so I have lost track of the date.

After I had coffee with Alita, I called my mother and I asked if she had my brother, Ed's cell phone number and she gave it to me. I hadn't talked to Ed, or we hadn't talked to each other in three years and I really miss him. We had been so close, even though his dad forbade him to have any contact with my sister, our mother and me. My call went straight to voice mail and I left Ed a message. I told him that I missed him very much and mentioned that I had left Jared.

Jared is one of the reasons my brother and I stopped talking. Once again a relationship I allowed Jared to ruin for me. Now I just have to wait and see if my brother calls me back.

I took a shower and for the first time in four weeks, I actually put some make up on, just a little mascara and eyeliner. I felt almost like a new woman. Funny how something so small, can make you feel so much better.

Margie Goldock called and told me my papers for my new driver's license had arrived, and my sister came to pick me up and took me over there. I took some new pictures and my sister had to identify herself and guarantee I was who I said I was, as I didn't have any identification myself.

My sister dropped me back 'home' and Inga was asleep when I got back. I checked that I had all the papers for my driver's license and put the picture in, now it was ready to be mailed. When Inga woke up, we had a cup of coffee and we were talking when my mother called and said that Jared had called her again.

He said if I only call him one more time, he won't bother me anymore. As always, my stomach started to hurt when I thought of him. Fear is getting to my nerves, but I'll call him.

We talked and agreed that I will pay $700 for our bills this month. I truly need that money myself but maybe Jared would cool down a bit if I helped him this time.

Once again, he begged to give him another chance. If I don't, he said I should keep that in mind that he actually begged me, but I said no.

"Please Jared, promise me that you won't do anything stupid."

But he remained silent. I told him that I took his silence as a threat to mean either I'd give him another chance or Jared would kill himself, but more likely kill someone else. Someone I care for and then I would have it on my conscious.

"No that's not what I meant."

I know it is and his next sentence confirmed what I thought.

"We will meet again, either in this life or the next one. I want you to keep in mind at that time that you said no when I begged you."

I had already given Jared so many chances and he had never proven to me that he could change. Why would it be different this time? It's too late.

He asked if there was someone else.

"No there is not, and never has been anyone else in my life but you. I've already told you but it just seems like you refuse to believe me."

And again, he asked me to call him at 10:00 p.m. and I said I would. Don't ask me why.

I was watching TV when my phone rang and to my big surprise, it was my brother Ed returning my call. When we first started to talk, he was short in his tone, but it got easier as the conversation progressed and we talked for about 45 minutes. I told him what had happen and about my plans to leave the country and go to the US. Ed said he would probably be going to California in February and in that case, we can have a chance to celebrate my 30th birthday together. That would be so wonderful!
He promised to call me again tomorrow and I can't wait to talk to him again. We hung up and I felt stronger than ever since I left Jared.

I called Jared back at 10:00 p.m. as I promised. He kept talking about my giving him another chance so he can show me sides of him I have never seen before. He said he would give me all the time I need to recover, and all freedom I wanted, if I just stayed with him.

I had given him fourteen and a half years of my life without him showing me he could treat me right. Why would I believe him now? There is only one person that can give me the freedom that I need, and that is me.

I will never again sacrifice my family and friends for anybody.

Jared was telling me that the only thing that stopped me from giving him another chance, was that I would feel ashamed for the people here, who filled me up with crap about him. He said he would respect it if I didn't give him another chance, but he will never accept it. It was a waste of time to talk to him and try to make him understand. I was feeling good when I went to bed and it feels like Ed gave me some strength today. Thank you my brother.

October 22, 1999

I opened my eyes at 8:00 a.m. and it was time to get up. I had coffee with Alita while I told her about the talk I had with my brother yesterday and how much that meant to me, also that it feels like Ed gave me strength just by calling me back. After that, I called my mother before watching *Days Of Our Life*.

The relationship Billie and Austin have, is the same type of relationship Ed and I had before. I would give so much to get it back. Inga and I were talking before she went out on the balcony to smoke when the pay phone rang and I answered it. It was Jared!

"I already told you, don't call on this phone."

Jared was depressed and needed to talk to me, he said.

At first, our conversation was okay, but then Jared started to ask me for another chance, but I told him that he knows where I stand. So once again, Jared told me to remember when next we meet, and sooner or later we will meet again, that he was begging me, as he expressed himself.

I must remember not to get angry at him now when he begs, because I will regret it. He never explained what he meant by that; he didn't have too. He knew that I understood. It doesn't matter how or what Jared says to me, everything is a threat in the end anyway. He tries to take control over my mind again and gets disturbed when it doesn't work. I told Jared how happy I was now after I took my freedom back and he sarcastically said,

> "You truly believe you took your freedom back? I gave it to you when I let go of you at the hospital, and I'm also the one controlling how much time it will last. I can find you whenever I want to."

"Stop threatening me like that, I'll call the police."

"There is nothing the police can do anyway to help you," I could hear how he smiled.

Oh, he makes me so irritated and drives me crazy. Just before we hung up, he asked if he, my mom and I can meet for coffee on Sunday.

"I already told you no!"

"Hm, call me tomorrow again. Talking to you makes me calm."

I said, "Okay," just to stop him from bugging me and we could hang up.

My mom came up around 5.20 p.m. and had picked up sandwiches for us, and I was looking forward to having my mom here tonight again. I told her about the conversation with Jared, and how difficult it is for me to talk to him. I don't want Jared to lose the apartment but at the same time, it makes me angry that he wasted all that money going to Spain. I didn't tell him to go there so it's not my fault, but Jared turned it around and told me that it is my fault, because I had been lying to him and hadn't told him where I was.

Anyway, it doesn't matter what I say to him. He has his own opinion and had already his mind made up.

Mother and Inga went to bed early, while I was up writing a letter when my phone rang. It was closer to 1.30 a.m. and when I answered, it was Ed; I thought he had forgotten about me. He apologized for not calling earlier and I told him not to worry about it; I was just glad that he called.

We talked for a few minutes and before we hung up he said,

"It's good to have my big sis back."

He melted my heart with that statement, and said we would talk again tomorrow. If he only knew how much talking to him means to me.

October 23, 1999

My mom came in and woke me up at 9:00 am, saying breakfast was ready. It was so nice to have her here in the morning, but still I felt anxious because of the way Jared is acting.

Inga left my mom and me alone, and once again, I started to talk about how frustrated this whole situation made me. I don't like that I have to give Jared any money, he's only trying to keep me from leaving. One thing is for sure, I won't let anything stop my plans. Now I just needed to wait and see what was happening with the Visa as I want to do this legally to make it as easy as I can for me.

My mother's boyfriend Patrick and his daughter came, picked my mother up at 2.30 p.m. and stayed to have coffee with us. I gave Patrick a house tour and he told me how sorry he was about my circumstances, and for all the bullshit Jared put me through all these years.

Yes, it is very sad and Jared wants me simply to forget about these years and that week! That last week . . . that horrible week when Jared just about killed me.

If I didn't put my hands up to protect my head when Jared swung the crunches, I would most likely not be here today, or I would be paralyzed. Those times when Jared raped me or forced me to do things I didn't want to do. How can I ever forget and forgive him for that?

Before they left I told my mother that if Jared called her to ask her to call me for him, she should tell him no, and that I don't want to hear about it. If she insists on telling me, I will change my number and not give her the new one.

When I set my bath water, my mother called again and said that Jared called just to see if I would call tomorrow as I promised? I quickly said yes, but I was so annoyed with my mother now. It seems like she doesn't take this seriously when I'm telling her I don't want to know if, when and why Jared calls.

Why is it so difficult for her to understand that it's just getting harder for me when I hear about him? When I get information about him all the time, how can I move on with my life?

I got in the bathtub and tried to relax as much as I could. Ed called and told me he was going out to party tonight, and I wished I could have gone with him.

I know I need to work on my self-esteem, but that is something I can focus on when I'm away from Sweden. Then I can start my new life.

I made dinner for us and it turned out delicious. The pay phone has been ringing incessantly, but no one responded when it is answered, and we know it's Jared calling. He wants to hear my voice before he responds, but it just makes me more determined when he acts like that, and I realize my only chance to stick with my decision and move on, is to stop talking to him. The only way to do that is for me to ignore everything from the life with him and start afresh. If I don't, it will altogether fall apart.

These 15 years, Jared had made sure to brainwash me to only listening to him, therefore every time I heard his voice or his name, it took me back to the time with him. I could hear him repeating: "No one can help you, no one can save you Hannah. You are mine forever."

It felt as if his soul got into me, like the movies when the devil is taking control over someone's body, and making them do things they don't want to do. Jared is eliminating who I am and it's eating me up from the inside. I'm trying to explain so the people around me understand, but either I can't and/or they don't get the picture.

I lost a filling in my tooth before I went to bed and need to go to a dentist and get it fixed. More money out, but it has to be done.

At the women's shelter, we are planning to go out to dinner November 12th and I can't wait to get out for a little while. It's probably my last time that I will be going out here in Sweden before the time has come to spread my wings and fly away.

October 24, 1999

My sister called and woke me up at 9.45 a.m. so I went up and out for a cup of coffee. I joined Inga on the balcony and my mind started to bring back bad memories, and suddenly my stomach started to hurt badly. Nervous tension I guess.

We talked about how I would have a normal life, and how nice it would be. While we talked, I remembered my last week at my house; how scared I was when Jared hit me with the crunch, he almost choked me and threatened me with the knife, both at home and in the car. How Jared had said—You want me to stick it in your chest?—How he pinched my ear so hard that it started to bleed and other horrifying things like that. It all came over me and I started to cry. Inga told me,

> "It's good for you to get it out, and at the same time, always think of that time if you ever came close to thinking of ever go back to him." She paused and continued, "Be happy you didn't wait until you're 65 years old to leave him."

"I wouldn't survive that long. Jared would kill me way before that."

My mom came up to visit for a little bit, and once again I told her how important it is that she actually hears me when I say I don't want to hear anything about Jared. I will move and change my number, won't ever talk to her again, if that is what it takes. I cried even more and I felt terrible now and times like this, it feels like I am taking one step forward and two steps back. Mom left and I was back to do nothing. I was bored, so I started to make dinner for us. It felt good as I hadn't been cooking much over the last three weeks, but the food turned out tasty anyway.

Later that afternoon, my mom called again and said Jared had been calling, to see if I could call him a little earlier and I said yes.

No one answered the house phone so I called his cell phone and got a busy tone. Anna who was here visiting came in and said a "Matthias" called on the payphone and asked for me, but before I took the phone, I knew it was Jared. He asked how I was doing and I was honest and said I feel terrible.

"Are you still keeping the promise to help me with money?"

"Of course but I've got an unexpected bill. I need to go to the dentist."

I explained what happened and I caught myself while I was doing it, there is no need to explain to him anymore. At least now I'm aware of that; it's a bad habit I've had for the past fourteen and a half years.

He said he had a gift for me, and just wanted to see me one more time before he leaves me alone.
"Just one more time and then I will let you go. You can live your life while I live mine, but make up your mind before my patience is over."

My first thought was, *'yeah, a bullet in my head the last time you see me?'* but I said,

"What will happen then?"

"Take a wild guess Hannah."

Jared sounded strange today and I got a very bad feeling. My gut told me something dreadful was about to happen. I wonder what he was up to. When he says things like that, I take it as a threat even if he denies it.

My whole body was shivering when we hung up and Jared had me extremely scared tonight. Why am I so frightened of him? That is because I know what crazy things Jared can do. I know how his mind works, and what can happen when he loses control. Anything can happen because he has a crazy person's mind and he truly is a lunatic!

My tears start to fall while I was walking out to the balcony and Anna came out to embrace and comfort me. My phone rang and it was Ed. He heard right away that something was wrong, and for the first time I told him about some of the awful things Jared had done to me. Ed called at the right time and told me before we hung up—

"If you have nightmares and wake up, always remember how much I love you."

My thoughts were running here and there and made me very confused, but I tried to focus on the conversation I had with my brother and how much stronger I feel when I talked with him. *'Thank you bro', for being here for me and helping me get over this crisis, the biggest in my life. You will always be with me wherever I go and I love you so much.'*

October 25, 1999

When I woke up at 8.45 a.m. my mom called, and we talked for a little while. It was time for me to get up and everyone here waits to have coffee until I wake up and make it, same thing this morning. The women here like my company and the shelter won't be the same without me. I took my coffee and kept Inga company on the balcony, we just sat there looking out over the city. It looks so pretty.

Jared called on the payphone and when I answered, he just said,

"Thank you for the money. How could you transfer the money without leaving the place you're at?"

I froze, how does Jared know I never left the apartment? I caught myself explaining to him, once again, and when I realized what I was doing I thought, *'stupid me, I never learn.'*

As the conversation progressed it got creepy, and it made me very terrified.
He said that he knows where I am now, and if I won't stop playing this childish game with him, he will stop it himself. I didn't believe he was telling the truth, so he said,

"You live in the same apartment complex as your sister but another number, and there is a strange name on the door." While Jared kept talking, my whole body started shivering. "I'm getting tired of giving you this freedom, and if you don't stop playing and solve this situation and come back home, I can't go on with my life. If you push it that far, it won't matter if we have thousands of people around us. I have let you go once, but not next time. It's your call Hannah."

"What do you mean by that?" I asked.

"I'm just saying, it is your call if we're going to have a happy or tragic ending. I'm going to follow you all over the world if that's what it takes for me to get justice."

Click. I hung up on him and cried like a baby when I was going in to Alita at the office.

My cell phone was ringing and when I answered, it was Jared again. This time I turned it off. How can he always get a hold on my cell number? I am so tired, because it's gone too far.

I called and spoke to the Officer Back but I didn't make any sense, I was so upset and said I would call him back.

I changed my number, again.

I spoke to my mom and told her what had happened and now she got mad at Jared. She called me back after a few minutes and told me she had spoken to Pauli. My mother had told her some of the things Jared had done to me, as she thought Pauli had the right to know why I left her brother. Pauli wanted me to call her back, which I did and she was upset how Jared had been treating me and felt so sorry for me. Her family didn't have any idea what had been going on at home with Jared and me and still she didn't even know *how* bad it had been. I was crying from time to time, and Pauli just listened and gave me whatever time I needed.

When I was done talking, Pauli told me that I will always be her kid's aunt and that they all love me. She said they would tell the kids whenever they thought the kids were ready, and that I will still be a part of their family, even if I'm not with Jared.

It felt like a rock fell from my heart finally to be able to tell her how terrible it had been for me. When we hung up, I felt a little stronger and relieved.

I called back to ISD's answer machine and left him a message; saying that I would think about it, but not promise to go to a therapist with him to get him help. Meanwhile, Jared is not going to call me, come looking for me, or even think of me, until I call him next Wednesday. After I did that, I felt better, now I was more angry than I was scared. That is good, because as long as I'm mad it's easier to deal with him and I'm just getting more determined.

I had the worst headache again, and I guess it was because of all things that happened today.

Every time I talk with Jared, he threatens me one way or another. If he doesn't say things straight out, I can just read between the lines. It is tearing me apart slowly, and I need to get it into my mind that Jared is not Spiderman or something like that.

I would never underestimate Jared though. He is smart and the reason he doesn't threaten me directly, is because he doesn't know if I am recording our conversations and would use it as proof in court.

I left Ed a voicemail with my new number and Annie came up to have coffee with me. Later when Inga and I were watching TV, my cell phone start ringing. When I answered, I heard it was Jared. How in the world did he get my number this time? I am going to turn the phone company upside down, this is just not right!

Jared asked if I had given any thought about talking to his therapist and I said of course, but the longer our conversation went on, I realized that he just wanted me to give him another chance. There is no way I will do that.

"I left a message at ISD's answer machine to leave me alone while I'm thinking about whether to talk to the therapist together."

"If you just give me only 1, 2, 3 weeks to prove to you that I have all these good sides, the ones you've never seen before, then I can live, knowing I did everything in my power to show you how much I love you. If you still want to leave after that, I'll let you go and live your happy and harmonic life while I do the same. But if you don't, then I will never get peace and can't let you have a peaceful and harmonious life."

Those were his words exactly and if that's not a threat, then I don't know what to call it. He kept on going, telling me not to involve other people in our business, like my sister and brother, and how Jared knew I had contacted Ed I don't know, because it would be sad if any of those I care for got hurt.

"Jared, are you threatening my family?"

"Oh no, I won't touch them. I just need to move my finger."

Nothing more needed to be said; just move his finger and pull the trigger. That is what Jared meant.

"Call me Wednesday and give me the answer about how you want your future to be, ok. If you don't give me this chance Hannah, my life is over, and then you don't have the right to live your life either."

When I went to bed that night, I was absolutely exhausted.

IT'S NOW OR NEVER

October 26, 1999

I still had a headache when I woke up and I didn't sleep well at all last night. I woke up from the slightest sound. Someone could have dropped a needle in the kitchen and I would have sat straight up in bed.

Alita was already there, and we had our morning coffee while we were chit—chatting about everything. They had finally fixed the internet so now I could send my e-mails. I took a shower and Annie came to pick me up and take me to Anne, my therapist. My sister had a friend with her, Rico who was Sahib's boyfriend. Rico was a good-looking guy, and it was nice to have something pretty to rest my eyes on in the car. While I was at women shelter, we don't see many people. I talked to Anne for about an hour and then it was back to the house again.

The day was quiet and for once, it was actually nice. Alita went home for the day, so it was just me and Inga left for the night. I got hungry and realized, we didn't have any food, so I called Annie to see if she could get me a few things from the store. Instead of coming up with the groceries she called me on the entry phone downstairs to let me know she was sending the groceries up in the elevator. I waited for a few minutes, to let the elevator come up, before I unlocked and open the door to get the food.
As soon as I opened the door, I see Jared come running down the stairs from the attic. I had no chance to shut the door before he pushed me into the apartment and came in after me. My heart stopped for a second and I thought my life was over.

I screamed to Inga—Jared is here—He grabbed my arm,

"I just want to talk to you, but first you're going to tell me where he is hiding. I saw the guy from downstairs."

Jared is insane and his look was crazy. There are no men even allowed up here. At this point, I was hysterical. He turned around and started walking in towards me. When I looked at the front door, it was still open and I remembered my sister was downstairs and shouting again.

"Annie he is here!"

Jared started to run into the apartment so I quickly ran the other way and out the door. I flew down the stairs as fast as I could. Tomas, my sister's other friend, passed me in the stairs as he was running up. It was dark, snowy and cold outside, but I didn't care. I didn't even have on any shoes, but all I was thinking about was, *'he just can't get me now, he just can't.'* This is about saving my life!

Annie was waiting down on the street for me and she grabbed me by my arm and dragged me into Sahib's store, locked the door and hid me in the back until the police came. My little body was shaking and when the female officer tried to talk to me, I could hardly speak. I tried my best to explain to her what happened, but I thought, *'Damn you Jared to mess things up like this.'*

The other cops went up and did a search in the entire place, but somehow Jared had already escaped. Annie gave me a cup of coffee in the store and the officers walked me up again, and around, just to show me that Jared wasn't there.

My sister was high and she was going crazy down there on the street, told her friends to look all over the area for him. My mom came with Patrick to make sure I was ok, but can't you people understand? I was not ok at all.

The police wrote a report about a stolen cell phone and illegal trespassing before the officers left. Jared had taken my phone but lost his own. He just destroyed everything for himself by doing this. All this time we had been talking, trying to find a solution and to work things out, has been a waste of time, and for what? Absolutely nothing. I figured out, there is no solution for this situation, only a solution for me. I have to leave my whole past and everything behind, and start all over in another country.

IT IS TIME!

Alita came back and she will stay with us tonight. We were up talking for a long time about what happened and I was the last one to go to bed.

Jared was calling his phone all night, but I didn't answer. I don't have anything to tell him anymore. I was so wound up I couldn't sleep, just lying in my bed to rest my eyes. Everyone had told me not to be scared up here at the women's shelter, and that Jared is not a Spiderman. Maybe now people can understand why I always have to sleep with one eye open.

October 27, 1999

Last night I didn't get any sleep at all, but I rested for about three hours and was totally exhausted when Alita came knocking on my door. She came in and we were talking for a while and after our talk, of course I couldn't go back to sleep. While I was making coffee, I thought about what happened last night. I wondered how could Jared be so stupid? Didn't he understand what damage he had done? Not only for me, but also to himself. I had tried to stay away and not talk to the police, but now it's out of my hands and there will be a report when other people are involved.

The atmosphere was terrible here today and I felt like everyone here was mad at me for what happened. That made me feel guilty even though I know it wasn't my fault.
Jared called me up on the pay phone and I told him I would talk to his therapist and tell him everything. We hung up.

I called the therapist right away and he was actually listening to me. Every now and then, I started to cry when I was telling the story to him. When next I spoke to Jared, our conversation was like a roller coaster. Sometimes he would sound somewhat normal, with as quick a turn around to his crazy talk, saying things that didn't make any sense. It was heavy talk and all the time I had to prove things for him and every other sentence Jared said was a promise and the other sentence a threat.

I am so tired of trying!

In the afternoon my bank contact, Larry Larsson called and said Jared had been there with an authorization to empty my bank account. The paper had my signature and Jared had also showed them my driver's license. I thought I was going to explode. Jared is out of his mind.

Fortunately, Larry didn't let him empty my account as I had been talking to them so often that the tellers knew better.

Time for another doctor's appointment and Annie came with two friends to bring me over to the hospital. They were waiting in the waiting room while I was in talking with my therapist. My sister had really been supportive and helpful lately.

The doctor put me on the sick list until November 14th and we will take it from there. He said to call if anything else happened.

Jared called almost as soon as I stepped into the apartment again. This time Beth and Alita didn't want to let me talk to him at all anymore, but I told them I'd make it short. He said he had been at my mom's house to drop off my cell phone and ID but she wasn't home.

Great, now I have to wait even longer on my personal belongings.

I went back in to my room and Alita came in and said she wanted to talk to me. She had a booklet with other women shelters and a bill for how much I owed for my stay and continued,

"We don't want to do this, but we are too scared to let you stay here anymore. You have to find another place to stay."

I was shocked, but at the same time I did understand, I just didn't understand why they blamed me. I spoke to Jared a few times and at night, Jared called the staff phone and terrorized them, so now there will be another report. Then Alita said,

"You can stay here tonight, but you have to leave tomorrow."

I was too tired even to be upset, while my sister freaked out, but there was nothing we could do. I packed the few things that I had and prepared for another good-bye tomorrow. I went to bed but I already knew it would be another sleepless night.

LIGHT AT THE END OF THE TUNNEL

October 28, 1999

My mom called me 8.50 a.m. to check on me and see how I was doing. As soon as we hung up Jared called me again on his cell. He told me to give him the money for the rent before I would get anything from him. According to him, now it's my time to show that I'm willing to oblige and work with him, not against him as I've been doing these fourteen and a half years. I couldn't believe what he said.

"Oh my God! Jared, you are just unbelievable."

I hung up the phone. I was so annoyed and upset with him and deep inside I knew I can never get my own life together as long as he was around.

No matter what I'm doing, I am damned if I do and dead if I don't!

Jared wants something he can't have and will not have—that is control over my mind and life again.

He kept on calling, so I turned off the phone and he started to terrorize the residents by calling the pay phone, so we temporarily disconnected it. They probably will have to change that number too because I gave the number to Jared, trying to prove to him how honest I am. My poor judgment, and my mistake.

I was fuming, but I knew what I had to do. I called The Flyaway Store.

"I need a one-way ticket to California."

"You can't buy a one way ticket to California, m'am, and if you are planning to stay longer than three month you would need a Visa."

"Okay so give me a three-month ticket then."

"When would you like to go?"

Damned if I Do, Dead if I Don't

"Tomorrow!"

The lady sounded surprised—

"Unfortunately we don't have a ticket to California for tomorrow."

"So when do you have the next available ticket? I want one as soon as possible."

"We have one a week from today."

"Okay I guess that is good enough. Ok so I want that one."

"And you are going to stay for three months, you said?"

"Yes I am."

But in the back of my mind I was thinking—I just need to get there.

I paid with my debit card and got a confirmation number. They were going to send the ticket to this woman shelter, and Alita promised me she would make sure I would get my ticket in time. She would send it to my new residence. I had no idea where I would go but Alita was helping me by calling other women shelters and there was a place in a town outside my city that would welcome me. This time I won't let anyone know where I am.

Alita called a cab for me and also arranged so I had a police escort to make sure no one was following me there. I asked the taxi driver to make a stop by the ATM, and I was chit-chatting with him all the way. He was actually nice.

When we got to my destination, Tasha who works there, came down to welcome me and help me carry my things in. There was another woman there also, and her name was Livy. I said hello to her before I got my room and started to unpack the few things I had. I in fact liked this apartment more as it was much nicer and my room a little bigger than the one I had at the first shelter. I called my mom and told her that I had moved but I didn't tell her where I was or what city I was in.

We were relaxing the rest of the day, talking and getting to know each other some more and sharing our life story.

I talked to Annie and called Ed but he didn't answer, so I left him a voicemail with my new number and told that I missed him.

Tasha went home at 6:00 p.m. and Livy went to bed early. I was by myself and for the first time since I left my house, I felt fine, as if I was at peace with myself. I wasn't as anxious as I was before, now that I knew I had a date to fly out of here.
Jared didn't have my number and no one knew where I am. I know I had made the right decision this time.

Now, it's 1:00 a.m. and time for me to get some rest. I haven't rested in a long time and I actually think I can relax enough to get some sleep tonight.

October 29, 1999

Livy knocked at my door 8.30 a.m. It was time to go up and call my doctor to see if he could extend my time on the sick list, and I also told him I was about to leave the country for a while. He told me it would be hard for him to put me on the sick list for any more time, so at this time I would have to draw from my unemployment. Now I really had to do some smart planning with my money.

I started to get anxious again, and had to calm myself down. I had already paid for my ticket and I had money for a new passport. That is all that matters. How I'm going to survive financially when I get there? Well, that's another question.

Livy had already made coffee for us and we had breakfast together. It's actually pleasant up here and once again, I was happy that I did change places and got away from the city.

I feel much safer here as no one knows where I am. 'If you don't know, you can't tell anyone,' a saying Jared used all the time. The only person I totally trust these days is myself. That is so sad but it's the truth.

I checked with my mom to see if she could call DMV for me and find out if they can hurry up with my driver's license, I needed it to be able to get my passport. I just have a week to get everything ready before I leave.

I got in the shower and for the first time in almost six weeks, I had a chance to get out all by myself, and I walked down to the mall. When I first stepped outside the door and thought I heard something, my heart jumped but after a little while I became calmer. It was so nice to be out, just be all by myself and breathe the fresh air. It was at the end of October so it was cold, but I enjoyed every minute of it.

First, I went to the ATM and then I was window-shopping. I smiled at everyone I saw thinking *'is this how it feels to be free? It feels amazing.'* I stopped by at a hair salon and had my hair trimmed. It needed to be done so badly and I felt like a new person when I left there. I have to be frugal with my money so I only bought a few things that I really needed; a pocket agenda, pen and paper so I can write, and a little English dictionary.

When I was ready to go back home I had two small bags to carry, but I didn't want to take the bus back now that I finally had a chance to be outdoors, so I walked all the way back. Once I came back, Tasha and Livy had start to become worried because I had been out for so long, but they also told me it took a lot of courage for me to go out by myself.

"You look really good Hannah. I can tell by your look, this day did you good."

It warmed my heart to hear those words. My cell rang and guess what? It was Jared!

"What does he do to get my number every time?" I said out loud and was very upset.

I hung up immediately and called my sister to tell her about everything that was going on. I asked her to call my father to see if he could call me back. I really needed to talk to him now.

My father called me right back and I told him what had happened.

"Do you have any plans as to what to do?" he asked.

I told him about California.

"Hannah, listen to me. It's almost Christmas and the New Year is coming. You know you can always come to Spain or go to my friends in Stockholm where you would be safe."

"No daddy, I won't! One thing I have learned by living with a "psycho", you can't fight Jared's craziness with talk and common sense. For me to feel safe in Sweden or Spain, would be to have a bodyguard, ready to lose his life for me, to follow me everywhere 24/7. That is no life, dad. I just have to get away to get peace in my soul to start over with my life."

My father didn't say anything more about it, just told me to call him before I leave. He asked where I am right now and I responded,—it is better if you don't know.

Annie called me back to see if she could do anything for me but I said

"No, but thanks for asking," I paused and said, "Actually you can give me Rico's number so I can call and thank him for helping me even though he doesn't know me."

"It's late Hannah, but you can call him. Rico is always up," and she was right. I told Rico how much I appreciated his help and support and how much it meant to me.

"Don't worry about it! No one should have to go through what you've been through and I'm just glad we could help."

"You know Rico, you guys are the only ones I trust enough to take me anywhere. I feel safe with you because I know you wouldn't let anyone come close to me. That's why."

"Thanks for trusting us and you're right, Jared will never get through to you as long as we are around."

Rico told me to call him or have my sister call him if I ever needed them.
I watched a little bit of TV and when I looked at the clock, it was already 2.30 a.m. It was time to go to sleep.

Good night everyone who is here to support me.

October 30, 1999

I haven't slept this good in forever! I woke up at 10.30 a.m. and I was well rested and full of energy. Livy had already made the coffee and was going down to the store, and I gave her money so she could buy me a new calling card. I put on the dishwasher, a load laundry before I got in the bathtub. I am not sure how or from whom Jared had gotten my other cell numbers, so to be on the safe side, I only gave this number to Annie. She must be able to reach me if anything changes.

I shaved my legs and painted my nails, something I haven't done recently. It was so nice to pamper myself again. I watched TV while I ate and then wrote a letter to my mom, one to my sister and one to Rico, just to explain to them how I felt and how much their help meant to me.

It was quiet here today and suddenly I started to get anxious again. I was worrying if Jared would find a way to stop me.

'No, it just can't happen! I won't allow it!'

I will never give him that pleasure of stopping me, ever again. *'Okay think, Hannah! Taking a taxi to the airport would be the best way out. Jared doesn't know where I am so he can't follow me. If he, on the other hand is keeping an eye on my sister, there is the possibility that Jared would follow her if they were coming to get me. On the other hand, if I took a taxi, I would be by myself and I needed them to keep me company and safe while I'm at the airport. I don't want to be all alone.'*

Well, I have a few more days to figure everything out, and I will definitely outwit Jared this time. I have to calm down again, otherwise I cannot think straight and won't get any sleep. I need all my energy and strength so I can follow through with this.

'Come on Hannah, you'll work this out. Just don't stress about it.'

I talked to Annie about my options and she didn't want me to take a taxi.

"You are more safe with us sis, I promise."

I have to think about it and do what is best for me. One good thing is that I am leaving so early and it will be dark outside, which means that it will be easier to see if someone is following us. *'It will be fine,'* I whispered to myself before I went to bed at 1.30 a.m.

October 31, 1999

I feel so much better up here than I did at the first shelter. Maybe it is because it's another city, or because I like the atmosphere here more. Livy and I clicked right away and we are like two little girls, giggling and talking. I got dressed and for once I was the first one up. I made coffee, and when it was ready, I took my paper and pen and started to write. I just emptied myself and my memory to leave room for the new.

When Livy came up I had another cup of coffee with her and Tasha called to check on us and make sure we were ok. I told her I was trying to figure everything out, it would be so much easier if I already had my driver's license and passport. I can't get a regular passport, only a temporary one that is only valid in three months, but honestly that is all I need. The best thing would be if I can do it without getting my sister involved, but I don't know if I can do it without her and the guys. I just don't want to get them involved more than I really needed to, because it puts us all in danger. My sister, Rico and Ronny jeopardized their lives too by being around me.

There was a program about abuse of women on the TV and I recognized myself in that program, all too well. They also confirmed what I said all the time, that it is as dangerous to call or go to the police. Most of the time, the woman is already dead when the police arrive and if not, the woman might never even press charges against the man, and then what happens next?

The men get even madder and the beatings get worse, or worst of all, the man kills the woman for 'messing' up his life. It's so twisted and wrong, but that is how their mind works. It's simply the truth.

Finally, my mom got a hold of Merissa and they are going to meet tomorrow so my mother can get my things and my sister can bring it to me when she comes to pick me up. When Livy went to bed and it was quiet, I finally started to write a letter to my dad. I was crying while I tried to explain for him how I felt, and why I made the decisions I made. Maybe I just should give him some of my poems as well. It is easier for me to express myself in writing my poems, than it is to talk.

My father says he wants to help me and I need his understanding and support more than ever. Maybe he can help at some point. I need my whole family more than ever at this moment in time. I gave Ed my new number but he hadn't called and it made me sad, and the only thing I can do is to pray he will call me another day. I fell asleep around 1:00 a.m.

November 1, 1999

My mom had called Annie to let her know my driver's license was there. Yes finally, now I can go and get my passport and then everything will be ready for my trip.
Tasha was already here, and when I stepped into the kitchen both of them said,

"Look who is here," and smiled.

I think I've become their little mascot. They just love to have me here and I'm happier than I've been in a long time.

My phone rang and when I heard it was Ed, my heart jumped as my brother makes me so happy. He had been out of town and apologized. It is okay, as long as he calls me eventually.

After that, my mom called and said that Merissa never showed up with my shoe and I just don't get it. Why make plans if you have no intention to show up.

Tasha, Livy and I walked down to the grocery store and it was nice to be out. I can't wait until I get to California where I can go out without being scared of the smallest sound around me, thinking it's Jared coming to get me.

We had a good time and when we got back, it was coffee time again. Just when we sat down Anne, my therapist, called me to see how I was doing. I told her I'm about to leave the country and she thought it was a excellent idea, which surprised me. I guess she figured out that Jared is extremely dangerous and I'm not safe here.

After Tasha left that afternoon, my dad called me and once again, I told him about my trip. My father was probably drunk the last time I spoke to him. He didn't remember too much of our last conversation and didn't say anything about my leaving for another country, other than he wants me to stay in touch with him regularly. Sounds like I have his support and again, I truly needed all the support I could get and especially from my family.

I ironed some of my clothes that I'm not going to wear before I leave, so I could start to pack. I don't want to wait until the last minute to get things ready. I need to focus on all other bits and pieces that needs to be done. I want the time to go a little faster so it will be Thursday and time to go. I went to bed and while I was lying in my bed I prayed to God.

> *Dear God. Thank you for protecting me and keeping me safe. Please give me the strength I need to build up my life again and to keep my family close to me.*
> *Thank you mom, dad, Annie, Ed, Anne, Rico and everyone who have had my back, and helped me to come this far.*
>
> *Good night everybody and I love you.*

November 2, 1999

The phone was waking me up and it was mom who called from Annie's phone, just checking in to see if I'm doing well. I stayed in bed but the phone out there was ringing, and it was Tasha who wanted to make sure I'm up. I called my doctor and when Tasha showed up, we had coffee before it was time to go and pick up my driver's license at the post office.

I put some make up on for once and Ingrid came to pick me up to take me to the post office. I looked like a completely different woman just in the few days I have been here. I got my driver's license and it turned out pretty good. Ingrid asked if I needed some new clothes? They have a cheap store not too far from here.

"Let's go and see if we can find anything."

I tried on some clothes and walked out with three new well-deserved outfits. When we came back, it was time for Ingrid to go home. I thanked her very much and gave her a big hug.

"Good luck, Hannah, and remember nothing is more important than your life."

She is such a nice woman. It is too bad, but I probably won't see her ever again even though she will forever be in my heart.

I started to think about my trip and stress out again. I don't have a place to stay when I get there, and I barely have any money, but I will figure something out.
I don't want to ask my dad for advice regarding my living, because I haven't told him I don't know where to stay. If I did, my father would have told me not to go and I don't need anyone trying to convince me that it's crazy. I already know it is, but I have to go.
Tasha took me downtown Gothenburg again, and my body tensed up as soon as we got close to the city. I tried to hide myself while sitting in the front seat, just in case Jared would pass us in a car or some vehicle.

I went into the police station and got my temporary passport, and then we headed back 'home'. On the way back, I felt better and we had such a good time together. Tasha is such a kind lady. It seems like I finally have the odds on my side, even if my nerves were trying to take over and play with my mind. This time it was not just fearing Jared, it was also excitement for the trip to another country and to my future.

Tasha had to leave as soon as we got back, so I said goodbye to her. She will be here tomorrow again. Unfortunately, I didn't have the chance to say goodbye to Livy as she had already left. Maybe it was the best that way. I am not very good at saying goodbye, and I just can't see the good in goodbye, because it always makes me cry. It feels like I am loosing everyone that I love. Either they leave me, or I have to turn my back at them, for my own good, and it's hard.

So tonight, I will be all by myself here, for the first time in weeks, but I think I'll be fine anyway. Tasha and I have so much to do tomorrow so it feels like the time is flying by. I spoke to my father and asked if he could tell me anything he thinks I should know about the USA. The only advice my father gave me was to stay out of trouble.

"Yeah, I will—and that's one reason I'm leaving Sweden."

My family knows I'm leaving in two days, but what they don't know, even though I told them a while ago, is that I'm not coming back.

I finished up everything and went to bed at 12.30 a.m. but was tossing and turning for a long time before I finally fell asleep.

November 3, 1999

I woke up at 7.45 a.m. and was so tired after only a few hours sleep last night. I went to the kitchen to make myself coffee, and while I was waiting for it to be ready, I started to clean out my stuff. It didn't take me a long time at all for the reason that all I had was a suitcase and a make-up bag. There is just no point in taking things I am not going to use. The day passed by pretty quickly and when Tasha finally showed up, I was so happy to get some company.

"How do you feel, sweetheart?" she asked me.

"I am getting anxious for tomorrow and couldn't sleep last night. I've been praying all night and all day that everything will go as I planned tomorrow.
Tasha, what if Jared somehow gets a hold on me? He told me, he just needs to see me one more time, and I know what that means. It just takes one more time to kill me."

"There is no 'if' Hannah! Jared is not going to find you. You'll be ok," was all Tasha said but her body language told me she was worried too.
When we sat down to eat dinner, neither of us said anything. It was so quiet and we knew what was coming soon; to have to say good bye!

It was time for Tasha to go and when she looked at me with tears in her eyes, I felt my own tears rolling slowly down my cheeks. My heart was aching and I couldn't find the right words to tell her how grateful I was to her and the other women who helped and supported me this past month. I might never see them again, but I know for sure, these women will always have a place in my heart. I waved to her from the window and saw her drive away.

Alita called me on my cell to let me know my sister had been there to pick up the few things I had forgotten while I was still living there, and more importantly, to wish me Good Luck.

"I will never forget you guys, and I will keep in touch to let you know how everything goes."

"You'd better," and I could hear she was smiling when she answered, but I also heard sorrow in her voice.
When we hung up the phone, I was thinking, *'I am actually leaving tomorrow, not for a day and not even a month. This time it's forever.'*
My nerves tightened even more when I started to realize tomorrow was the day. My last chance to escape this zany man before he finds and kills me.

It was now 7:00 p.m. and even though I was so tired, I knew I couldn't sleep. I checked and rechecked for the last time that everything was packed, my travel clothes were out, my passport was in my purse and, oh yeah, my money too. *'Okay Hannah, everything is ready and packed, so relax.'* That was easier said than done when all I was thinking was—what if something goes wrong tomorrow, then my life is over. It can either be the last day of my life, or the very first beginning of a life.
This is the last day in the country where I was born and raised, my last day as a prisoner, and my last day in this living hell.

I jumped when my phone rang and interrupted my thoughts, fearing that it would be Jared. *'Hannah, stop it, everything will be fine. He doesn't have your number,'* I told myself before I answered.

It was Patrick, my stepfather, who wanted to say goodbye to me and when we were done, it was time to speak to my mother. She tried to be strong for me and not shed tears, but her voice broke and gave her away.

"Mom, don't cry, you know I'll be ok," but deep down I questioned it myself. I went on, "Whatever you do mom, don't talk to anyone at your job about me. Absolutely nothing! Not that I left or that I'm out of town, and definitely not where I am going. You know how they like to gossip and I can't afford, not even, one mistake."

"I promise I won't tell anybody. If I get any questions, I don't know anything about where you are or what you are doing. Take care, my angel and call me as soon as you can and when you are safe. Remember that mama loves you so much; you are always in my heart. Your sister just left and she told me to tell you to call her in the morning to get the directions from you. Oh, my little baby girl, I miss you already."

"I love you too, mom." I hung up.

I was crying and crying hard. I don't know when I will see her or even if I can see and talk to her again. This wasn't the way I had planned my life. I have to run away to save my life, but I just know it's better to be far away and alive, than to stay here and end up at the cemetery or even worse, at the bottom of the ocean where no one would find me. There is no other way out than this.

The fear I feel for him is deep, and I would forever looking over my shoulder wherever I go or wherever I am. I could, of course, go to my dad in Spain, but it's too close. I know Jared was going to look for me there, and he proved me right two weeks ago when he drove down there just to look through my father's house.

My father wasn't even home, only his wife. My father was in the hospital. Jared didn't believe Liza when she said I wasn't there. Neither of them, had a clue about what I was planning to do, because I hadn't told them, until I told my dad the other night. I know they would try to talk me out of it and talk some 'sense' into me, say it is insane and crazy to run away like that. Liza just doesn't know how it is to live in total fear; to every day wake up and wonder what kind of mood he will be at today. Every day scared to be absolutely crushed, and wondering every day if this will be my last day to be alive.

I just refuse to keep on doing this. Enough is enough! I'll do whatever it takes to get myself a nice and quiet life with no drama. Is that too much to ask?

It was 1:00 a.m. when I pulled out a pillow and a blanket. Maybe I can to go to sleep on the couch but even when I was so tired, there was no chance I could rest at all. I was way too hyper! At 3.30 a.m. I called Annie and gave her directions to where I was, so she, Rico and Ronny, could come and pick me up and take me to the airport.

The reason I asked my sister and her friends who are all doing drugs, instead of the therapist with whom I talked a few times, is because I knew if Jared showed up somehow, he would have to kill them to get to me. My sister can do a lot of bad things, but she would never let him get to me as long as she is there. I realized with Jared, that you can't fight craziness with reason, only with craziness!

It will take them a while to get here, so I got in the bathtub and did my best to relax at least a little while, before it was time to go. My emotions were in chaos with everything from excitement to fear. From time to time, I felt as if I was on my way to my own execution. Who knows, it might be, only time will tell. I am not safe yet!
I got dressed and put my things by the door and then all I had to do was to wait until they got here. Just another hour, but it felt like a long, long time.

November 4, 1999

At 4.40 a.m. my cell rang again, this time it was Rico, to tell me they were here. He asked if I wanted him to come up and help me with my luggage, I accepted and told him how to get up here.

Last check, bathroom and bedroom, I hadn't forgotten anything. I turned off all the lights, locked the door and put the key in the mailbox.

All three of them were high and tired, which was understandable. I thanked them all for doing this for me. They were the only people I could feel comfortable and relaxed with while I was still in Sweden.

While we headed for the airport, I looked over my mail while I sat in the back seat. My new phone card was here and that was important. I gave my sister $25 and I know it wasn't a lot, but I didn't have much money for myself either. I didn't want them to just leave me at the airport in case Jared had followed us, and for that reason they parked the car and walked me in. All I had was one suitcase and one bag to check in, so it went fast and we start to walk up to the customs.

Once again, I had tears rolling down my cheeks when I turned around and gave Rico a big hug.

"Thank you so much Rico, it means so much to me. Take care of yourself, okay."

"It's all good, baby girl; you are a very strong and brave young lady. Keep your head up and you'll be okay."

I gave his friend Ronny a hug too and said thank you once again.

My sister and I have had many fights and argued so much in our life, but to stand here and say good-bye to her, not knowing when or if we will ever meet again, made me forgot about all those times. We were hugging each other and I whispered in her ear

"I could never have done this without you sis and I love you."

"I love you too Hannah. Now I just want you to go and get yourself a good life and happiness. No one deserves it more then you."

That was the last time I saw my sister. Just to make sure, I asked the customs agent who checked the passport, if they were allowed to come in with me, but no this was it!

To go pass that area everyone needs to have a ticket. My sister, Rico and Ronny were waiting for me to keep on going and for the doors to close. Now I was all by myself. While I was sitting there waiting to board, I was looking around at all people and thinking *'I would not be surprised if Jared showed up here,'* but fortunately he didn't.

They called my flight, and we had to take a bus out to our plane. I was one of the first ones to actually board the plane and found my seat. I buckled up but was still frightened and kept my eyes on the entrance until they closed the doors.

When the plane started to move, I felt relief. It was like a big stone, actually more like a whole mountain, fell from my heart. Now there is no turning back and there is no looking back.

This is the beginning of a new life! *My life!*

Right after we took off I fell asleep, but just for a few minutes. I woke up in time to get some breakfast. Then we landed in Paris, where I changed planes for the flight to California. That is when I started to relax a little more. I had a few hours between the flights and I took that time to make some telephone calls. My mother was first on my list and she was so happy to hear my voice. After I hung up from her, it was time to talk to my father. Now was the time to tell him my plans; that I had left Sweden for good, because I finally got the courage to get up and leave Jared.

My father had come home from the hospital and was drunk when he answered, which didn't surprise me. What I didn't tell him, was that I didn't have any plans as to what I would do, I didn't know where to stay when I got there, but it didn't matter. It sounded like he didn't listen to me anyway, or maybe he didn't care. He just told me to call him when I got to California, to let him know I got there safe and tell him how to reach me. I couldn't tell him I only had my ticket and that was it. I was not coming back!

I really didn't want to tell too many people where I was going, because the more people who knew, the bigger the risk that someone would slip if Jared asked, and he will ask, believe me. Time was flying and it was time to board the flight to California.

Wow! This is a big plane, the biggest one I have ever been in,' I thought. But then again, the US is a big country.

I felt like a little girl that was running away from home, and in one way, I guess I was. I had never been on a plane for that many hours either, but that was the purpose of this journey, to get as far away from him as I could.

I felt how tired I was now when I had relaxed some more, and I was lucky not to have anyone on the seat right next to me. My ankle was a little bit sore too, so I lay out on both seats and fell asleep. I woke up two hours later from someone tapping my shoulder, *'Jared is here,'* but it was just one of the flight attendants asking if I wanted something to eat or drink.

"No thank you, I am fine."

When she left, it all came over me again. Not only how I had just left my whole life behind, but also the entire obsession Jared had with me, and how close he came to killing me.

I had no clue what life has in store for me, but I was alive and I know that it is now that my life really begins. I will be 30 years old in a few months, but it is never too late for a change or to start a new life. I read my letters from my mother and my sister again, and this time all I felt was warmth. I realized all they want for me is for me to be happy, no matter what it takes, even if it has to be on the other side of the earth.

I dozed off again with a smile on my face, and suddenly I am back when Jared, my sister and I flew the last time. It was in August this year, after my dad's birthday. Jared pretended to be in a good mood, even though he was acting like a real jerk towards Annie and me when we drove to the airport because we had to pay a toll on one of the roads and, of course, my sister and I could have prevented this, according to Jared. The toll was only 750 pesetas or $1.

"Just throwing our money away, but what else can I expect from two retards?"

I know what you are thinking, but that is how his way of thinking.

I quickly opened my eyes again, and looked around and slowly I realized where I was. It was just a memory, a very bad memory. I was happy that I had found the strength to get up and go, finally to leave him, even if it took almost 15 years and I had to leave everything behind.

Once we got closer to land, I started to be excited and scared too. Where am I going to stay, and how do I get there? I started to stress myself out again and thought—*'oh well girl, you just have to wait and figure it out when you land.'*

I was absolutely amazed of the size of the airport, and smiled when I was thinking that I thought Paris airport was big. It was now 3.30 p.m. Pacific time, but I was still on Swedish time, which was 12.30 a.m., already a new day.

There was a lot of paperwork to fill out and I started to feel anxious. I just wanted to get out of the airport right now, and figure out which hotel I would go too.

As soon as I got my bags and saw all the people who were there, waiting on the relatives and friends from my flight, I suddenly started to feel lonely and lost. *'I will feel better after I have settle down and get some rest at the hotel,'* I thought, but oops, I didn't even have a hotel to go to. I looked around and went to the information desk, asked about hotels close by. The lady gave me a big binder with lots and lots of hotels, and she could probably tell I was lost.

She looked at me and said, "Remember, you get what you pay for." I didn't even know where the different cities were, or if the neighborhood is good or not as good, or anything. I found a Holiday Inn, at what looked like a good price, at least for tonight, so I called and booked a room.

First thing in the morning, I need to find something cheaper because I knew I was going to run out of money very fast. All I had was a total of $250 in my name and won't get any more money, another $250, until another two weeks. The lady at the desk, told me there is a shuttle which will take me to the hotel, and as soon as I got there, I said thank you to the driver, checked in and got my key. When I got to my room, I felt the tiredness coming over me. I got undressed, could still see some of the bruises on my body, and relived to be here, away from him, I got in the bathtub.

When I closed my eyes I almost fell asleep, so I dried off my body, put the towel around my hair and laid down under the cover.

For the first time in many years, I could lay down with peace of mind, knowing Jared is not going to bother me tonight and I fell asleep as soon as my head touched the pillow.

Facts

- 1 in 5 high school aged girl reports being victim of verbal or physically or sexually abused by a partner they're dating. 80% of teenage girls who has been abused stay in the relationship, and only 33% tell someone.

- Every year, 5.3 million women are abused; more than three women are murdered by their husband or boyfriend only in the US every day.

- Domestic Violence injures more women every year than rapes, muggings and car accidents combined.

- A woman increases her risk of being killed by 75% when attempting to leave an abusive home.

- One of every six pregnant woman is beaten, making Domestic Violence a leading cause of birth defects.

I also want to point out when it comes to Domestic Violence, there is no "stereo-type" for an abuser or a victim. They can be in any shape, race, size, age, social class or religion.

If you are in an abusive relationship remember, it's NEVER your fault. Leave the first time it happens, don't believe when he says "it'll never happen again," you can't cure him with your love. Leave and do whatever it takes to get away from him; if you need to move to another city, don't hesitate. It's about to save your life! There is people out there to help, don't be afraid to ask. At women's shelters they help, listen, comfort and most important, there is people who understands.

Abuse is about power, and when you talk about the abuse he start to lose his power; when you leave, he loses the power.

Are you, your daughter, niece, friend or someone else you know abused? If anyone you know show signs of abuse, don't be afraid to ask them about it. If they are avoiding the question or hesitating with their answer, ask again. There are always signs, if we only look.

Please remember: Living with someone who abuses you is the same as playing "Russian Roulette," next time might be the time you'll be one in the "murdered" statistic. Don't be afraid to ask for help. There is help and solutions out there. I wish you the best luck!

In case of an Emergency call 911 in the US, outside the US dial your countries emergency number or

The National Domestic Violence Hotline
1-800-799-SAFE (1800-799-7233) or
TTY 1-800-787-3224

www.thehotline.org